T0208295

Eternal Security On Trial

Deconstructing One of the
Most Misunderstood Doctrines in the Church Age

Andrew G. Robbins

authorHOUSE®

AuthorHouse™
1663 Liberty Drive
Bloomington, IN 47403
www.authorhouse.com
Phone: 1 (800) 839-8640

Published by AuthorHouse 09/06/2019

ISBN: 978-1-7283-2642-9 (sc)
ISBN: 978-1-7283-2641-2 (e)

Print information available on the last page.

Dedication

To everyone who never believed everything they were told without first thoroughly investigating all the facts. This book is dedicated to those noble individuals, like the Christians of old in Berea, who study the Scriptures every day for themselves to see whether or not what their pastors and instructors are teaching agrees with God's Word.

Dedication

To everyone who never believed everything they were told without first thoroughly investigating all the facts. This book is dedicated to those noble individuals, like the Christians of old in Berea, who study the Scriptures every day for themselves to see whether or not what their pastors and instructors are teaching agrees with God's Word.

Thanks and Acknowledgments

A special thanks to my editor, Sherry Weir, who I now call "Eagle Eye Sherry" for her ability to spot problematic areas in written communication. Thanks, Sherry, for an amazing job.

Acknowledgments to Dr. Jerry King, my friend and mentor, who has taught me about the Kingdom of God in a way I never previously understood. You are an amazing gift to the world.

Bible Translations Used

Unless otherwise indicated, all quotations from the Bible come from the New International Version (NIV).

All capitalized and italicized font in the scriptural quotations were added by the author for emphasis sake.

Contents

Introduction

How This Book Came to Be

In my travels in business over the last 25 years, I have been privileged to meet many kinds of people with widely different backgrounds and beliefs. I have had associations with many claiming either no faith at all or whose beliefs are a hodge-podge of humanistic intellectualism and mysticism. Even among Christians who attend church regularly, I have found the interpretations of certain Bible doctrines to vary greatly.

Many years ago, I had a client who was and is an exceptionally godly man. He has a delightful, jovial personality and endeavors to be about the Father's business by doing whatever he can to make disciples for Christ. As we chatted over lunch one day, the subject came upon his extended family. He began talking about his brother who was not living a Christian life and whose sordid behavior and poor life choices had strained family relationships, inflicting great damage on his own life and the lives of others. I extended whatever sympathy I could. "I'm so sorry to hear that," was about all the comfort I could offer.

He responded with a remark that took me aback a little: "Well, at least we will be together in heaven someday, and then everything will be alright."

I couldn't resist pressing a little. "What do you mean?"

"Well, he was saved early in his life, but he's just not living out his faith."

I bit my tongue and redirected the conversation. Part of me wanted to unload a double-barrel of biblical buckshot on him, but another part of me didn't want to rob him of the comfort his theology provided regarding his brother. Yet, I knew that comfort was based on false hope. For that reason, perhaps I should have opened the conversation about his views on eternal security. But it was a business meeting, and I didn't think it was the time or place. Looking back, however, someone's salvation hung in the balance, and perhaps it would have been the decent thing to do to at least plant a few thoughts for him to mull over.

Prior to that day, the subject of unconditional eternal security had come up on a few occasions in both business and ministry settings, the most memorable of which were the sermons my wife and I were hearing at the Baptist church just outside Indianapolis we began attending in the late 90's. We were hearing concepts preached I had never before been exposed to, such as the idea that once a person is saved, he/she will always be saved no matter what. I was raised in Assemblies of God and non-denominational churches, all of which taught that the believer's salvation was a conditional offer. These new teachings were therefore very surprising to me and in stark contrast to the teachings I had grown up hearing. I began wrestling a little with these new doctrinal positions, and being a man of the Word, I wanted to investigate them for myself.

I should point out that as I began diving into the Scriptures on the subject of eternal security, I didn't do it hoping to prove someone wrong. This was during a time in my life when I was questioning many of the doctrinal positions and church customs I had cut my teeth on, and was, in fact, hoping to disprove some of those practices I found intellectually troubling. Therefore, I had no bias. I just wanted to know for myself. So, for five weeks straight it was all I studied. During that time, after a particularly nasty back injury had left me bedridden for several days, I did nothing all day long for hours at a stretch but read and study on this topic while propped up in my bed. It turned out to be one of the most enlightening times of my life. I came away from that five weeks no longer confused. I was convinced that I had found what the Bible really says about the conditionality of our salvation. I began furiously putting down notes and eventually came up with the first version of the book you are now holding.

My Thesis in Summary

I am a rather black-and-white person, but I acknowledge that there are some grey areas on the topic of unconditional eternal security. While the Scriptures are replete with passages on almost every page clearly demonstrating the free will God has granted us, there are also passages forcing us to wrestle with some elements of divine predetermination. Therefore, it's somewhat understandable why some people would lean hard toward a more fatalistic (the belief that everything is predetermined and therefore unchangeable) predestination theology, while others lean hard in the other direction toward undirected, autonomous, and totally independent choices. I do not believe either of these extremes is correct.

On that note, I haven't met a single Christian who falls into the second camp of believing our lives are totally autonomous. The only people I have ever met who believe that are atheists, and atheists are not my target audience for this book. My target audience is the other extreme – the camps who believe we are powerless to change our destinies because every detail of our lives has supposedly already been pre-determined, as well as those who hold that a Christian's salvation has already been established and is thus unchangeable regardless of what we do or believe. While this treatise will put those doctrines to the test, I will do so while acknowledging the mysteries of God and the unexplainable elements of a Being Who exists outside of time, space, and frail human logic. In doing so, I will further acknowledge the small degree of healthy tension between the two schools of thought due to the mysteries about God we will never fully comprehend this side of eternity. In the words of the *Got Questions.org* webpage describing Calvinism vs. Arminianism, "Ultimately, it is our view that both systems fail in that they attempt to explain the unexplainable. Yes, God is absolutely sovereign and knows all. Yes, human beings are called to make a genuine decision to place faith in Christ unto salvation. These two facts seem contradictory to us, but in the mind of God they make perfect sense."

It is my contention that there is a certain amount of predetermination *and* free will mysteriously existing in God's Kingdom simultaneously. We should not assume God does not direct our lives in some respects, nor should we assume God has removed from us the element of free will and the resulting blessings or consequences of our actions. Since the former view has little following in Christian circles but the latter is widespread, we will deal with the fatalistic way of interpreting the Bible and demonstrate the conditionality of our salvation and a more Scriptural understanding of the sovereignty of God as it pertains to eternal security.

Some Introductory Thoughts

Many other books which thoroughly deconstruct unconditional eternal security have already been written. Upon reviewing the choices of reading material on the subject, one can be nearly overwhelmed by the volume. Books, articles, and websites abound on eternal security, both pro and con. Such a vast body of information may make it seem redundant and perhaps even a little presumptuous to offer yet another book on the subject. However, for some busy folks it may be beneficial to offer a broad overview hitting only the high points. Our discussion, therefore, will simply address some of the most common arguments pertaining to the doctrine of unconditional eternal security. (For more exhaustive works on this topic, I recommend Dan Corner's books, which can be found on Amazon or other similar outlets.)

I also wish to make clear from the start my desire to avoid appearing divisive in addressing this all-important subject. I address it for the sake of exalting Scripture and attempting to do my part in perhaps bringing resolution to a disagreement that has already brought much division in the Body of Christ. I am willing to take the risk of offending some of my brethren because I see the doctrine of eternal security as potentially fatal for some. It is for this reason the concept of unconditional eternal security has been called one of the worst heresies in all of Christianity by some notable leaders today; it offers backsliders false hope even as they drift from the teachings of our Lord while comforting themselves in their belief that their eternity is still secure in the decision they made once upon a time to serve Him. Concern for these individuals motivates me as well.

There are some doctrinal controversies probably better left alone for the sake of unity among the brethren. This is not one of them. While some minor doctrinal issues make little difference in our eternal destiny (such as whether or not to use music in the church, or whether or not baptism should be performed by immersion or sprinkling, etc.), the issue of unconditional eternal security may make or break the salvation of some people.

Some people who adhere to this teaching are clinging to the doctrine of eternal security as their ticket to heaven. They may have once prayed a prayer of repentance to God and were at the time sincere. They may have gone through the waters of baptism and remained in fellowship with other believers for a time but then began to be enticed by the pleasures of the world. Slowly, their hearts began to be hardened to the conviction of the Holy Spirit and to the Word of God. They began indulging their sinful pleasures to the point of living in blatant and gross sin and feel no shame or remorse, much like the brother of my client I mentioned earlier. They feel no compunction to return to their "first love" because they felt secure in their false belief that their salvation is secure because they once prayed a "sinner's prayer" and were baptized. For them, the issue is not which of their many sins caused them to lose their salvation. We all fail in many ways, and there is no one sin which will cause a *repentant* person to lose their salvation. Rather, it is a *lifestyle* characterized by gross and unrepentant sin, or an abandonment or renunciation of the faith causing the downfall.

For the diligent and obedient disciples of Jesus, eternal security is not even an issue. Let me be very clear: All who cling to the Savior in a love relationship characterized by a lifestyle of faith demonstrated by obedience are eternally secure (see James 2:15-26). *Nothing can rob them of that salvation as long as they cling to the Savior.* For these faithful ones, regardless of what they believe about eternal security, their salvation is unshakable.

Therefore, I am *not* speaking here of a salvation so fragile that if you explode in a fit of rage, for example, you would suddenly be outside of God's grace. Some people on the opposite extreme of the issue believe if a person died immediately after committing a sin, he/she would lose their salvation and go to hell. That concept, still taught in some Christian circles, is not found in the Bible. What I will be speaking of throughout this study is a salvation which the Bible teaches is contingent upon a lifestyle of faith – a faith which expresses itself through a desire to please God and walk in His ways as a matter of lifestyle. A particular one-time sin cannot forfeit the salvation of one who truly loves God and is struggling to live a holy lifestyle; however, a life of unrepentant disregard for God and His ways can.

Lastly, allow me to reiterate that I love all my brothers and sisters in Christ regardless of their stance on the eternal security doctrine. Many who believe in unconditional eternal security are faithful followers of the Word of God and live good and pure lives. I hope to maintain a spirit of love and unity even while addressing this difficult and sensitive issue. We all need one another, and division within the Body can be just as disastrous as false teaching. However, I realize the very attempt to topple the sacred cow of unconditional eternal security will of itself appear somewhat divisive, since attempting to discredit a theological camp many hold so dear may be regarded as offensive by some. While unity and love are important to me, unity for unity's sake is not my chief aim if it compromises the Word of God.

Therefore, I hope you will read on with the same attitude in which this book was written – in a spirit of concern, love and goodwill toward all who truly love the Lord Jesus.

.

1

A Side-by-Side Comparison of Calvinism and Arminianism

In order to understand the doctrine of unconditional eternal security, or what is sometimes referred to as the "once-saved-always-saved" doctrine, we have to know a little about the history and doctrinal framework from which it emerged. It might also be helpful to have some knowledge about the opposing doctrinal camp to Calvinism, called Arminianism.

Eternal security, the way it's being taught today, sprang up during the Great Reformation, in part, from the teachings of John Calvin, a prominent figure in Geneva in the 1500's. Today, an entire doctrinal camp called Calvinism, otherwise known as Reformed Theology, makes up about two percent of churches in America according to research conducted by noted church historian and theologian, John Gerstner, as presented in his series on church history. The reason it's not more than two percent is simply because most Christians and pastors apparently do not buy into this doctrine. That two percent nevertheless represents a fairly significant number of churchgoers.

Arminianism is the name of a doctrinal camp which seeks to explain the relationship between God's foreknowledge and mankind's free will, especially as it pertains to salvation. Arminianism is named after Jacob Arminius, a Dutch pastor and theologian who also lived during the 1500's in Amsterdam. His teachings are best known for their counter-arguments to John Calvin's theology.

Arminianism emphasizes the responsibility and free will of mankind in our relationship to God, while Calvinism teaches divine predetermination of mankind's actions, something Martin Luther referred to as "bondage of the will," meaning that no one truly has free will because all of our actions have been prearranged by God.

Both doctrinal positions are summarized with five points, as follows.

1.   The Depravity of Mankind

Calvinism holds to the position of mankind being totally depraved and incapable of choosing God on his own, while Arminianism teaches that mankind is indeed depraved but is nevertheless capable of choosing or rejecting God's grace. Arminians believe there is still a degree of goodness in mankind since we are made in the image of God and have a God-consciousness built into us. Made possible by God's grace, the sinner is being drawn to Christ and has the God-given ability to choose salvation.

2.   Unconditional Election vs. Conditional Salvation

Calvinism includes the belief that salvation is unconditional, thus the term unconditional eternal security, or unconditional election, meaning it cannot be revoked even if a person turns away and renounces what he/she once proclaimed. Arminianism believes in conditional salvation, emphasizing perseverance of the saints in the faith. Unconditional election is the view that God pre-determines and therefore orchestrates salvation based entirely on *His* doing, not on anything the individual has done or even believes, and therefore, there is nothing an "elect" person can do to prevent or undo that salvation. Arminianism, however, asserts that God grants salvation to people based on the exercising of their free will to choose God. Those who hold to a more Arminian theology of *conditional election* do not deny God has foreknowledge, but within the context of that foreknowledge there is granted mankind the grace of free will, and with that free will mankind can indeed choose God only to later reject Him and forfeit the free gift of salvation.

3. Limited Atonement vs. Unlimited Atonement

Calvinism teaches that the atoning sacrifice of Christ is not available to the whole world but limited to only a group of people pre-selected by God. Arminianism sees grace as unlimited, meaning Christ died for the whole word. "Limited atonement" is the belief that Jesus died only for the elect. "Unlimited atonement" is the belief that Jesus died for everyone, but His death is not put into motion in the life of an individual until a person receives Him by faith.

4. Irresistible Grace vs. Free Will

Calvinism holds the belief that God's grace is irresistible, meaning a person pre-selected to salvation has no ability to reject the grace of God since they were pre-determined to receive it in the first place. Arminianism believes an individual has the free will to resist and ultimately reject the grace of God.

5. Perseverance of the Saints

Both Calvinism and Arminianism teach "perseverance of the saints" but differ starkly in how this term is understood and applied. Perseverance of the saints in the context of Calvinism refers to the concept that a person who is elected by God will persevere in faith and will never permanently deny Christ or turn away from Him. Arminianism's position is believers in Christ can, of their own free will, turn away from Christ and thereby lose salvation; hence, a condition of salvation is persevering in one's faith.

As with many doctrinal camps, there are slightly different variations of belief in both Calvinism and Arminianism. Many believers maintain a mixture of the two without even knowing it. Indeed, most casual churchgoers have probably never even heard the terms, Calvinism and Arminianism, and if they have, fewer still truly understand what they are and what each position teaches.

While we will not deal with each of the five points one-by-one since our focus is unconditional eternal security, the following chapters will touch on all five points and examine each one from the pages of God's Word.

For our purposes in this chapter, however, let's take a closer look at one of those five points.

The Depravity of Mankind

It's important to understand this point before we begin deconstructing unconditional eternal security point-by-point since this area provides a foundation upon which we will better understand what Calvinists believe about "election" (i.e. the ones chosen or elected by God, referred to as the "elect" of God).

As already pointed out, Calvinists believe mankind is so totally depraved that we have no ability to choose to accept God's grace and would never do so on our own, and therefore, God must pre-select people whom He programs to receive His grace. They use as their basis for this belief the third chapter of Romans where the Apostle Paul writes:

> [10]*As it is written: "There is no one righteous, not even one. [11]There is no one who understands, no one who seeks God. [12]All have turned away; they have together become worthless; there is no one who does good, not even one."*

Two things must be pointed out as we seek to understand Paul's words.

First, these are not actually Paul's words, but he is quoting from the book of Psalms, chapters 14 and 53.

Secondly, as with many places in Scripture, Psalms is noted for its frequent use of hyperbole, or justified exaggeration in order to emphasize a point. When Psalm 14 is read in its entirety, it becomes obvious the Psalmist is using this method of poetic hyperbole to describe the sin into which the Jewish nation had fallen.

For example, Psalm 14:4 says the workers of iniquity "eat up my people as they eat bread." It's clear the Psalmist is not describing cannibals who *literally* eat God's people. Rather, this is a hyperbolic and poetic way of describing those who live without regard for God and who are crushing and devastating God's people.

This same hyperbolic method is often used in the book of Psalms and is found throughout the passage in question in Romans 3 as Paul quotes from the book of Isaiah as well.

David, the Psalmist who penned Psalm 14, was not suggesting the workers of iniquity can never do anything good. He was simply using justified exaggeration to illuminate on the folly of their ways. It is likely the Apostle Paul, who was a former Pharisee and who knew the Old Testament Scriptures by heart, understood this and was making a similar point. His quotation from Psalm 14 is not a fatalistic declaration about the total depravity of mankind but rather a statement about how Jews, too, are prone to sin, just like the Gentiles, and all of mankind stands guilty before God as sinners and needs a Savior. He takes lethal aim at the high-minded Jewish elitism that led to the belief of their salvation being secure simply for being born Jewish. Look at the context in Romans 3:

> *What then? Are we [Jews] any better? Not at all.*
> *For we have already made the charge that Jews and*
> *Greeks alike are all under sin. (v. 9)*

Ultimately, Paul states, "*All* have sinned and fallen short of the glory of God" (Romans 3:23). Therefore, while Romans 3 does not teach Total Depravity, it does emphasize the universal nature of mankind's sinfulness regardless of heritage and that there is no privileged position or special status in God's sight, not even as God's "chosen people." Paul, who loved his fellow Jews and said he would be willing to die for them, preached emphatically that Israelites are sinful just like the Gentile people whom they considered "unclean." All people groups are equally in need of God's deliverance and justification, which He offers liberally through Jesus Christ to all who call on His Name. That was the entire point of Paul's words in Romans 3.

It must also be pointed out that Romans 3:11 – *There is no one who understands, no one who seeks God"* – is not only **not** a statement about man's inability to respond to the grace of God, but it must also be measured and counterbalanced by the nearly-countless statements in the Bible which says humans can and do seek God, such as...

> **⁶Seek the LORD while He may be found; call on Him while He is near. ⁷Let the wicked forsake their ways and the unrighteous their thoughts. Let them turn to the LORD, and He will have mercy on them, and to our God, for He will freely pardon.**
> **-Isaiah 55:6-7**

> **You will seek me and find me when you seek me with all your heart.**
> **-Jeremiah 29:13**

> **This is what the LORD says to Israel: "Seek me and live..."**
> **-Amos 5:4**

Let us also consider that we can see there is God-given goodness in mankind, even among those who have not made Jesus the Lord of their lives, just by observing the actions and accomplishments of others. There are millions of people from all walks of life who have contributed in various ways to the good of mankind. Such inborn goodness does not qualify anyone for salvation, of course, because salvation is not based upon our merits but on faith alone, though we see the fingerprints of God even on ungodly people.

On September 11, 2001, for example, when the World Trade Center in New York City was attacked, we witnessed the selflessness and bravery of fire fighters and other first responders who risked and indeed gave their lives in order to save others. Many of these husbands, wives, sons, daughters, and friends from all walks of life had no religious reason to do what they did. They were not motivated by faith, because many of them claimed no faith other than perhaps a general belief that God exists. Yet there was something in them – something good – which moved them to risk and sacrifice their lives for others.

We see another example of some degree of innate goodness in the lives of even people who reject God demonstrated very clearly Mark 10:17-22 with the rich young man who approached Jesus asking about how to achieve eternal life. Jesus responded to his question by listing several of the Ten Commandments, to which the young man responded, "Teacher, all these I have kept from my youth." And the Scriptures tell us Jesus looked on him and "loved him."

This young man was a faithful Jew, a keeper of the Law of Moses. He wanted to know God yet stopped short when he saw what it was going to cost him. He walked away from that conversation with the Lord still in his sins. But Jesus nevertheless saw goodness in him and loved him for it. Also notice Jesus offered that young man the opportunity to be His disciple, leaving the decision in his charge (free will). If that young man was unable to respond to grace because he was predetermined by God to reject the Messiah and die in his sins and go to hell, Jesus would have known that and declined to offer him a place of discipleship in the first place. If the rich young man was predestined for hell, Jesus would not have bothered answering his question. He would have said, or at least thought to himself, something like, "Sorry buddy, you're bound for hell and there's nothing either one of us can do about it." Rather, Jesus wanted him to choose for himself the way of life, extending the offer to accept or reject.

Let's remember we were *all* created in God's image according to Genesis 1:27. Sin didn't change that. We are still God's creation, even though we are now all tainted by sin. As God's creation, all people have a God-awareness built inside of them which makes everyone conscious of God's ways even when they choose to reject Him. The Apostle Paul speaks of this in Romans 1.

>*[18]The wrath of God is being revealed from heaven against all the godlessness and wickedness of men who suppress the truth by their wickedness. [19]For what may be known about God is plain to them, because God has made it plain to them. [20]For since the creation of the world God's invisible qualities, His eternal power and divine nature, have been clearly seen, being understood from His workmanship, so that men are without excuse.*

The rest of Romans 1 goes on to describe the various expressions of wickedness which can result from pushing one's self away from the truth of God, but nowhere does it suggest wicked people have totally lost the ability to know God. To the contrary, it says what may be known about God is already evident even to the rebellious, because God has made it known.

These examples from God's Holy Word are irreconcilable to the doctrine of unconditional eternal security, which leans heavily on the Calvinistic tenet of the total depravity of mankind. According to this view, man has no ability to choose God for Himself, and therefore God must choose who will be saved apart from the moral choice of the individual. Therefore, it follows that this sort of salvation cannot be and will never be revoked no matter what the individual chooses to do or believe. If that sort of salvation actually exists, then yes, there would be no changing it. We can see clearly from God's Word, however, mankind does choose to respond to God or reject Him, and therefore the salvation He offers is contigent upon persevering in the faith, which we shall examine in more detail in later chapters.

2

Can a Christian "Fall from Grace"?

What does it mean to "believe"?

In the gospel of John, there are several well-known verses in which the word *believe* appears. John 1:12 says the following:

> *But as many as received Him, to them He gave the right to become the children of God, even to those who believe in His name.*

Likewise, the famous John 3:16 declares this:

> *For God so loved the world that He gave His only begotten Son, that whoever believes in Him should not perish, but have eternal life.*

John 11:25 follows suit:

> *I am the resurrection and the life; he who believes in me shall live even if he dies...*

In all three passages, as well as elsewhere in the New Testament, the Greek word translated into English as *believes* or *belief* is the present active participle *pisteuo* (pist-yoo-oh). Pisteuo literally means "to cling to; to adhere to" and implies a *continual* belief that bears fruit in one's actions and lifestyle.

Belief in Christ that results in one's salvation, therefore, is characterized by a desire to conform one's life to His precepts and principles **on a continual basis** and does not result merely by a general sense of agreement or performing a one-time ritual. In other words, it's not enough to just agree that Jesus is the Son of God. If you love Him, Jesus said, you will desire to keep His commandments (see John 14:15). On a related note, it's also not enough to simply undergo a confirmation process in one's church or be baptized or kneel down at an altar and have someone declare you to be "saved." Even if a person has performed any or all of these ceremonial exercises, without a desire to walk with the Savior and follow in His footsteps then salvation has not been experienced.

What are we to believe, therefore? *How* do we come to that belief, and *in whom* are we to place our belief?

The message of the whole of Scripture is that mankind is sinful and we have willfully and repeatedly violated God's Holy Law. There is no good in us which would merit pardon of our crimes by God, and all are under the wrath of His judgment. Apart from Christ, Who was God's representation of Himself on earth and Who took the punishment meant for mankind so we could have a way of escape, no amount of good works or moral conduct would ever be enough to appease God's judgment against sin.

We must recognize and acknowledge, therefore, our corruption in thought and in deed, and that sin has separated us from God. We must likewise believe in Jesus Christ as the only way to receive forgiveness from the Father, understanding and accepting Him as the substitutionary sacrifice for our sins. Furthermore, we must repent for our sins if the previous beliefs are to be consummated. Repentance means we turn from our previous lifestyle of sin and seek a life of holiness in conformity to the will of God described in Scripture. When we place our faith in Christ, we are exonerated of our guilt and declared children of God who will enjoy an eternity in His presence after this earthly life is done. It's this same faith that always results in a progressive transformation inwardly and outwardly.

This, in a nutshell, is the gospel.

Apostasy in the Galatian Church

The Apostle Paul was a champion of salvation by grace. His entire ministry was characterized by his revelation that salvation cannot be obtained by observing the Law; he proclaimed that salvation by law-keeping means one must observe the entire Law – all 613 Old Testament laws – without even the slightest sin throughout one's life. The Apostle James followed suit when he wrote in James 2:10 that if we fall short in even one part of God's Old Testament laws we are guilty of breaking all of it. Therefore, if a person is going to rely on moral conduct as assurance of salvation one must measure one's conduct against all 613 Old Testament laws, not by comparing one's self to other people. Since we all fall short, however, there is no hope to experience salvation based upon moral conduct or keeping the Laws of God.

Jesus Christ, however, came as God's representation of Himself upon the earth, and took upon Himself the punishment for sin, even though He never sinned. As Second Corinthians 5:21 declares,

> *God made Him [Jesus] who had no sin to be sin for us, so that in Him we might become the righteousness of God.*

This paved the way for mankind to have access to God despite our sins, as long as we humble ourselves before God by admitting we are sinners and not deserving of His grace and by placing our faith in Jesus Christ as our only way to heaven.

This is the gospel Paul preached. He went to great lengths to instill in the hearts and minds of his converts the principle of salvation by grace alone. Therefore, it was especially distressing to Paul that some whom he had discipled were turning again to a salvation message emphasizing certain observances of the Law. The Christians at the church in the Roman province of Galatia were one such example. Paul was so troubled about the church in Galatia turning again to a salvation-by-works observance, he addressed a letter to them which has been immortalized in the book of Galatians.

The entire basis for the writing of the letter to the Galatians was Paul's concern for the eternal souls of those who were being deceived by a false gospel. In the letter, Paul states both in essence and literally that those who observe any other gospel than the one he had preached were cutting themselves off from the grace of God. In fact, in Galatians 5:4, Paul wrote:

> **You who are trying to be justified by the law have been alienated from Christ; YOU HAVE FALLEN AWAY FROM GRACE.**

Bear in mind that these are **Christians** Paul is addressing. One cannot "fall away" from something one was not bound to in the first place. For example, great chunks of ice that fall off of glaciers and float away are no longer part of the glacier because they *fell away.* They become isolated from and are no longer a part of the glacier. Similarly, Paul was warning those whom he had converted to the Christian faith but who were now attempting to adhere to Jewish standards of law-keeping for salvation, saying they had isolated themselves from the salvation of God and had fallen away from grace.

Those who contend that it is impossible to lose salvation once a person receives it often claim that churchgoers who appear to be living a righteous life and then leave the church and turn to a life of sin and self-indulgence were not really saved in the first place. However, such an argument does not consider Paul's very clearly admonition to the Christians in Galatia warning them of the danger of *losing their salvation* if they continued to mix in a salvation-by-works message into what he had already taught them. The people Paul addressed in his letter to the Galatians were believers, that's clear. In verses 8-11 of the fourth chapter, Paul writes:

> *8Formerly, when you did not know God, you were slaves to those who by nature are not gods. 9But now that you know God – or rather are known by God – how is it that you are turning back to those weak and miserable principles? Do you wish to be enslaved to them all over again? ...11I fear for you, that somehow I have wasted my efforts on you.*

Continuing with this theme, the apostle Peter likewise addressed this when he wrote in Second Peter 3:19:

> *...be on your guard so that you might not be carried away by the error of lawless men and FALL FROM YOUR SECURE POSITION.*

Both Peter and Paul warned Christians to adhere to the true gospel lest they forfeit their salvation. Not that God would strip them of their salvation, but they would forfeit it in exchange for a false and damning doctrine.

Consider also that if it is impossible for the righteous to be led astray after they have received salvation, why did Paul once oppose Peter and essentially say both he and Barnabas were practicing hypocrisy and had been "led astray?" Paul wrote about this unpleasant scene in Galatians 2:11-13:

> *11When Peter came to Antioch, I opposed him to his face, because he was clearly in the wrong.*

> *¹²Before certain men came from James, he used to eat with the Gentiles. But when they arrived, he began to draw back and separate himself from the Gentiles because he was afraid of those who belonged to the circumcision group. ¹³The other Jews joined them in his hypocrisy, so that by their hypocrisy even Barnabas was led astray.*

Thankfully, these devout men of whom Paul speaks were humble enough to accept his rebuke and repent of their hypocrisy and go on preaching and living according to the true gospel. However, it is clear from the context throughout the book of Galatians that even devout men like Peter, who had actually been at the feet of Jesus, were in danger of forfeiting their salvation because of a fear of men which led to a subtle perversion of the gospel message. If it is possible, therefore, for devout men like Peter and Barnabas to fall into a false gospel and potentially forfeit their salvation, and if it is possible for people who had been discipled by the great Apostle Paul himself to fall from grace, how much more should you and I tremble at the possibility of hypocrisy existing in our own hearts. We should therefore do as Paul instructed and *examine yourselves to see whether you are in the faith; test yourselves.* (2 Corinthians 13:5).

Paul also wrote to the young pastor Timothy and warned:

> *The Spirit clearly says that in later times some will ABANDON THE FAITH and follow deceiving spirits and things taught by demons.*
> *-1 Timothy 4:1*

The word *abandon* in 1 Timothy 4:1 is the Greek word *aphistémi*, which means to *lead away, to depart from, to leave or withdraw.*

Once again, one cannot abandon what one has not been joined to in the first place. You cannot leave or withdraw from something you were never part of or connected to. Paul didn't say people would *reject* the faith in the first place, although we know that is also true. His obvious inference here is some who are *in* the faith – Christians – will one day **depart** from it and thereby forfeit their salvation, because instead of following the true gospel, they are deceived and adhere to doctrines taught by demons.

A similar warning can be found in Matthew 24:23-24 where Jesus spoke to His disciples about latter times.

> **²³Then if anyone tells you, "Look, here is the Messiah," or, "There he is," don't pay any attention. ²⁴For false Messiahs and false prophets will rise up and perform many miraculous signs and wonders so as to deceive, if possible, even God's chosen ones. See, I have warned you.**

If it was not possible for God's people to fall away and be deceived, why did Jesus feel it was necessary to give this warning about the end of times? Can we take Jesus' warning to mean it is indeed possible for a person to genuinely come to faith in Christ, and then change what they believe and thereby fall away from grace (i.e. to forfeit their salvation)?

Further evidence supporting the possibility of Christians falling away from grace can be found in the book of Acts. The Greek word *dechomai* (dek-om-ahee), which was translated into English as "received" in various places in the New Testament when referring to people who *received* the Word of God (Acts 8:14, 11:1, 17:11) and which means *to accept,* is the same word Jesus used to describe the people in Luke 8:13 who "received" the word with joy when they heard it, but because they had no root they "believed" (*pisteuo* – the same word used in John 3:16) for a little while and then fell away during times of testing. The people Jesus described in Luke 8:13, therefore, received the Word in the same manner as those who were being saved in the book of Acts, and they believed in the same manner described in the book of John as a condition for salvation; yet Jesus Himself said these people fell away.

This leads us to the question as to whether or not sin in a person's life can cause one to forfeit his or her salvation.

3

A Conditional Offer

Those who hold to a "once saved, always saved" doctrine often refer to Ephesians 2:8-9.

> **[8]For it is by grace you have been saved, through faith – and this is not of yourselves, it is the gift of God – [9]not of works, so that no one can boast.**

This verse is undoubtedly fundamental to the Christian experience and the teachings of how one receives salvation. When read in the context of the whole of Scripture, though, there is nothing to infer one cannot forfeit the free gift of salvation through unbelief. In fact, the verse itself suggests otherwise. This very verse declares salvation is a gift of God **through faith.** Salvation is only available to those who receive it by faith, and it is only people who hold fast to that faith who should feel eternally secure. We have already seen from the book of Galatians that Christians who for some reason begin to doubt they can be saved on the merits and sacrifice of Jesus alone and who begin to turn instead to Law-keeping, place themselves once again under the curse of the Law, the final result of which is eternal destruction.

James, the brother of our Lord Jesus, who was the no-frills author of the letter bearing his name, declares unequivocally that faith without corresponding action is no faith at all; it cannot save anyone. Here, we go back to the English rendering of the Greek word, *pisteuo* – a belief which manifests itself in action on a continual basis – as found in the book of John. James reiterates that mental assent to the Lordship of Jesus and the fact that salvation comes only through Him is not enough. Faith must demonstrate itself in action or else it is not faith at all.

> **14What good is it, my brothers, if a man claims to have faith but has no deeds? Can such a faith save him... 17Faith by itself, if it is not accompanied by action, is dead. 18But someone will say, "You have faith; I have deeds." Show me your faith without deeds, and I will show you my faith by what I do. 19You believe that there is one God. Good! Even the demons believe that – and shudder.**
> -James 2:14-19

While it must be abundantly clear that salvation cannot be obtained based upon one's actions, since *all have sinned and fall short of the glory of God* (Romans 3:23), it must also be abundantly clear that the faith which causes one to take hold of the free gift of salvation is a faith resulting in fruit in one's life; not just for a little while but all through one's life.

The first and most conditional fruit of faith is repentance, for without repentance, there can be no salvation. Paul wrote, "*Godly sorrow brings repentance that leads to salvation*" (2 Corinthians 7:10), and it was Jesus Himself who said, "*Unless you repent, you will perish.*" In fact, it was in the same passage of Scripture where Jesus also told a sobering parable:

> *⁶A man had a fig tree planted in his vineyard, and he went to look for fruit on it, but did not find any. ⁷So he said to the man who took care of the vineyard, "For three years now I've been coming to look for fruit on this fig tree and haven't found any. Cut it down! Why should it use the soil?" ⁸ "Sir," the man replied, "leave it alone for one more year, and I'll dig around it and fertilize it. If it bears fruit next year, fine. If not, then cut it down."*
> *-Luke 13:6-9*

It is apparent from this parable that God is looking for fruit from those who claim to love Him. After He gives a Christian ample opportunity to produce fruit, yet there still are no signs of it, then according to Scripture that Christian may be cut off from the Kingdom of God.

Jesus addresses this issue again in the book of John when he said:

> *⁵I am the vine, you are the branches. If a man remains in me and I in him, he will bear much fruit; apart from me you can do nothing. ⁶If anyone does not remain in me, he is like a branch that is thrown away and withers; such branches are picked up, thrown into the fire and burned.*
> *-John 15:5-6*

Jesus' words were actually preceded by the wilderness preacher, John the Baptist, who prepared the way for the Messiah. John once declared:

> *⁸Produce fruit in keeping with repentance...¹⁰The ax is already at the root of the trees, and every tree that does not produce good fruit will be cut down and thrown into the fire.*
> *-Matthew 3:8, 10*

Again, the first and most fundamental of the fruits God is looking for is repentance. One cannot come to God and receive His salvation at all unless he first sees himself as morally bankrupt and undeserving of eternal life. It makes a mockery of the sacrifice of Jesus on the cross to see one's self as a fairly good person who must be generally pleasing to God already because of his/her good moral standing in the community, or because he/she "would never hurt anyone." Repentance means seeing one's self in truth and grieving at the sight of it; it is being broken over one's sin to the point we share the pained lament of King David when he prayed:

> **¹Have mercy on me, O God, according to Your unfailing love; according to Your great compassion blot out my transgressions...³For I know my transgressions, and my sin is always before me. ⁴Against You, You only, have I sinned and done what is evil in Your sight, so that You are proved right when You speak and justified when You judge...¹⁶You do not delight in sacrifice, or I would bring it; You do not take pleasure in burnt offerings. ¹⁷The sacrifice of God are a broken spirit; a broken and contrite heart, O God, You will not despise.**
> **-Psalm 51:1-4, 16, 17**

Repentance demonstrated by brokenness over one's sins and a desire to walk in the ways of God are one of the conditions of salvation. Once again, this is not to be a one-time event at the time of saying a "sinner's prayer" or entering the waters of baptism. Repentance, like faith, is a *lifestyle*.

Jesus' very first sermon demonstrates the importance of brokenness over sin.

> **³Blessed are the poor in spirit, for theirs is the kingdom of heaven. ⁴Blessed are those who mourn,**

for they will be comforted... [8]*Blessed are the pure
in heart, for they shall see God.*
-Matthew 5:3, 4, 8

Jesus is speaking here of those who see themselves as morally bankrupt – poor in spirit; who grieve over their sinful condition – those who mourn. Anything less than this kind of acknowledgment of one's sins is not genuine repentance. This kind of repentance leads one to desire purity in the inmost parts, and those who lose such a desire and allow themselves to turn back to a lifestyle of habitual, willful, and unrepentant sin can also forfeit their salvation.

Let us examine this truth in more detail.

4

The Consequences of Willful
and Unrepentant Sin

The Apostle Paul's letter to the Christians in Rome, as recorded in the Book of Romans, was clearly written to those in the faith; and yet, Paul declares in chapter 8, verses 12 and 13, those who live according to the sinful nature will die. It is obvious he was not talking of unregenerate people here, since all through the previous verses in chapter 8 he speaks to the fact that those who are "in Christ" are free from the power and control of sin. Yet, he goes on to say:

> *¹²Therefore, brothers, we have an obligation –*
> *but it is not to the sinful nature, to live according*
> *to it. ¹³For if you live according to the sinful nature,*
> *you will die; but if by the Spirit <u>you put to death the</u>*
> *<u>misdeeds of the body</u>, you will live.*
> *-Romans 8:12, 13*

In other words, we who have experienced salvation through faith in Jesus Christ are no longer under the control of sin. We now have the power to resist temptation's pull. We have been regenerated, and since we are free, we have an obligation to use our freedom to put to death the sinful deeds of the body and live in holiness. If we do nothing, however, and instead *allow* sin to continue to control us, living in the same sinful habits we did before we were in Christ, then we will once again become a slave to it and die. Paul likewise points out in the sixth chapter of Romans, verse 16:

> *Don't you know that when you offer yourselves to someone to obey him as slaves, you are slaves to the one whom you obey – whether you are slaves to sin, which leads to death, or to obedience, which leads to righteousness?*

The writer of the book of Hebrews likewise makes plain that Christians can and often do fall into judgment because of continual sin:

> *[26]Dear friends, if we continually keep on sinning* **AFTER WE HAVE RECEIVED A FULL KNOWLEDGE OF THE TRUTH,** *there is no other sacrifice that will cover these sins. [27]There will be nothing to look forward to but the terrible expectation of God's judgment and the raging fire that will consume His enemies. [28]For anyone who refused to obey the Law of Moses was put to death without mercy on the testimony of two or three witnesses. [29]Just think how much more terrible the punishment will be for those who have trampled on the son of God and have treated the blood of the covenant as if it were common and unholy. Such people have insulted and enraged the Holy Spirit who brings God's mercy to His people. [30]For we know the One who said, "I will take vengeance. I will repay those who*

deserve it." He also said, "THE LORD WILL JUDGE
HIS OWN PEOPLE." *[31]It is a terrible thing to fall into*
the hands of the living God... *[12:14]Try to live at peace*
with everyone, and seek to live a clean and holy life,
for THOSE WHO ARE NOT HOLY WILL NOT SEE THE
LORD.
  -Hebrews 10:26-31, 12:14 (NLT)

This passage is not difficult to decipher. God's grace covers the repentant ones who trust in Jesus as their savior. Christ's sacrifice, though, does not cover those who continue to live in direct disobedience to the commands of God. *"There is no other sacrifice that will cover these sins."*

Jesus also speaks unambiguously in Matthew 10:33 about those who disown Him:

> *Whoever disowns me before men, I will disown*
> *Him before my Father in heaven.*

The word translated into English as *disown* is the Greek word *arneomai,* which means to *deny, disavow, or repudiate*. Repudiate means to refuse to fulfill or discharge an agreement or obligation. Thayer's Greek Lexicon states *arneomai* is used to describe followers of Jesus who, for fear of death or persecution, later deny Jesus as their master, and desert His cause.

For one to disown something, one has to have ownership of it in the first place. One cannot disown something that was never his to begin with. If a person *disowns* Jesus, it implies he/she was once with Him, only later to reject Him as the disciple Peter did when confronted after Jesus' arrest. If someone disowns Jesus permanently, Jesus speaks plainly that He will disown such a person in eternity.

I once heard a story which perfectly illustrates disowning Jesus. A small group of Christians were holding secret church services in a communist nation that had outlawed all forms of

Christian worship. During one such secret gathering, two armed soldiers stormed through the doors and barked, "Those who are not willing to die for your faith can leave right now!" Several of the worshippers got up and ran out, but several others stayed to take what they thought was going to be their last stand for Jesus. After the cowardly departed, the soldiers put down their weapons and said to those who remained, "You may continue. We just wanted to separate the sheep from the goats before we worshipped with you."

Did you know God says COWARDS will have their share in the lake of fire?

> *⁵He who was seated on the throne said, "I am making everything new!" Then He said, "Write this down, for these words are trustworthy and true." ⁶He said to me: "It is done. I am the Alpha and the Omega, the Beginning and the End. ⁷To him who is thirsty I will give to drink without cost from the spring of the water of life. He who overcomes will inherit all this, and I will be his God and he will be my son. ⁸BUT THE COWARDLY, the unbelieving, the vile, those who practice magic arts, the idolaters and all liars – THEIR PLACE WILL BE IN THE FIERY LAKE OF BURNING SULFUR. This is the second death.*
> *–Revelation 21:5-8*

Who are the cowardly? According to Scripture, the cowardly are those who ultimately disown Jesus because they thought their comfort during times of testing or persecution was more important than standing fast; *and* those who behave a certain way while with their church friends but behave very differently with their worldly friends for fear of being ridiculed or ostracized. These are the ones Jesus said He would disown and would be cast into eternal torment. Just in case the early Christians forgot the words of Jesus regarding this issue, Paul made sure to reiterate them in his letter to the young pastor Timothy:

> *If we endure, we will also reign with Him. If we disown Him, he will also disown us...*
> *-2 Timothy 2:12*

The warning that one can forfeit one's salvation is reiterated countless times throughout Scripture. Here are only a few examples:

> *If I tell the righteous man that he will surely live, but then he trusts in his righteousness and does evil, none of the righteous things he has done will be remembered; he will die for the evil he has done.*
> *–Ezekiel 33:13*

> *[17]If some of the branches have been broken off, and you, though a wild olive shoot, have been grafted in among the others and now share in the nourishing sap from the olive root, [18]do not boast over those branches. If you do, consider this: You do not support the root, but the root supports you. [19]You will say then, "Branches were broken off so that I could be grafted in* [speaking of God's rejection of the old Jewish system and of His making salvation available to the Gentiles]. *[20]Granted. But they were broken off because of unbelief, and you stand by faith. Do not be arrogant, but be afraid. [21]FOR IF GOD DID NOT SPARE THE NATURAL BRANCHES, HE WILL NOT SPARE YOU EITHER. [22]Consider therefore the kindness and severity of God: Severity to those who fell, but kindness to you, provided that you continue in his kindness. Otherwise, you also shall be cut off.*
> *-Romans 11:17-22*

> *By this gospel you are saved, IF YOU HOLD FIRMLY TO THE WORD I PREACHED TO YOU. OTHERWISE, YOU HAVE BELIEVED IN VAIN.*
>   *-1 Corinthians 15:2*

> *I am afraid that just as Eve was deceived by the serpent's cunning, YOUR MINDS MIGHT SOMEHOW BE LED ASTRAY from your sincere and pure devotion to Christ.*
>   *-2 Corinthians 11:3*

> *[19]The acts of the sinful nature are obvious: sexual immorality, impurity and debauchery, [20]idolatry and witchcraft; hatred, discord, jealousy, fits of rage, selfish ambition, dissensions, factions [21]and envy, drunkenness, orgies, and the like. I WARN YOU AS I DID BEFORE, THAT THOSE WHO LIVE LIKE THIS WILL NOT INHERIT THE KINGDOM OF GOD.*
>   *–Galatians 5:19-21*

This is a useless warning, by the way, if Paul's Christian readers cannot fall away from the faith.

> *[7]Do not be deceived: God cannot be mocked. A man reaps what he sows. [8]THE ONE WHO SOWS TO PLEASE HIS SINFUL NATURE, FROM THAT NATURE WILL REAP DESTRUCTION; the one who sows to please the Spirit, from the Spirit will reap eternal life.*
>   *–Galatians 6:7,8*

> *[19]My brothers, IF ONE OF YOU SOULD WANDER FROM THE TRUTH and someone should bring him back, remember this: [20]Whoever turns a sinner from the error of his way will save him from a multitude of sins.*
>   *–James 5:19-20*

¹⁹...[A] man is a slave to whatever has mastered him. ²⁰IF THEY HAVE ESCAPED THE CORRUPTION OF THE WORLD BY KNOWING OUR LORD AND SAVIOR JESUS CHRIST AND ARE AGAIN ENTANGLED IN IT AND OVERCOME, THEY ARE WORSE OFF AT THE END THAN THEY WERE AT THE BEGINNING. ²¹IT WOULD HAVE BEEN BETTER FOR THEM NOT TO HAVE KNOWN IT AND THEN TO TURN THEIR BACKS ON THE SACRED COMMAND THAT WAS PASSED ON TO THEM. ²²Of them the proverbs are true: "A dog returns to its vomit," and, "A sow that is washed goes back to her wallowing in the mud."
     -2 Peter 2:19-22

The aforementioned verses point us to a different conclusion than eternal security. The eternal security doctrine uses verses that are ambiguous in comparison.

But let's now examine the verses commonly used to defend the eternal security doctrine.

5

A Close Scrutiny of the Tenets of Eternal Security

Some who oppose the teaching of eternal security proclaim in no uncertain terms that the doctrine is one of demons – a subtle twisting of the gospel, laying waste to the standards of holiness and giving license for living in continual and unrepentant immorality. Yet, it is easy to see why sincere Christians who earnestly desire to do and believe righteously would believe such a doctrine if they took passages that appear to support eternal security and did not interpret them in light of the whole of Scripture. In other words, one must never take a handful of verses isolated from their context and attempt to build a theology around them.

For example, there is a verse in the book of Proverbs which reads: *Though a righteous man falls seven times, he rises again.* Whenever I have heard this verse quoted, it has always been used to describe how a truly righteous person may fall into sin from time to time but will always rise back up and continue in a life of righteousness. But look at this verse in context with the verses before and after:

> ^{14}**Do not lie in wait like an outlaw against a righteous man's house, do not raid his dwelling place; ^{15}for though a righteous man falls seven times, he rises again, but the wicked are brought down by calamity.**
> **–Proverbs 24:14,15**

As you can see, the *context* of this passage has nothing at all to do with falling into sin. It is referring to a righteous man appearing to be repeatedly decimated by trouble and calamity, but ultimately rising back up each time because God is looking out for him. The old saying, "You can't keep a good man down," may have come from this verse.

Just as some well-meaning people have isolated one verse from this passage in Proverbs and quoted it to imply something other than its true meaning, likewise others have taken passages and read into them a doctrine of eternal security without interpreting them against the backdrop of the rest of Scripture.

With this in mind, let's examine the primary pillars of Eternal Security. There are nine tenets to consider, and we'll examine each based upon Scripture and context.

Tenet #1
"Nothing, even our own wills, can separate us from the salvation of Christ"

> ^{35}**Who shall separate us from the love of Christ? Shall tribulation, or distress, or persecution, or famine, or nakedness, or peril, or sword? ^{36}As it is written, For thy sake we are killed all the day long; we are accounted as sheep for the slaughter. ^{37}Nay, in all these things we are more than conquerors through him that loved us. ^{38}For I am persuaded, that neither death, nor life, nor angels, nor principalities, nor powers, nor things present, nor things to come,**

> [39]*nor height, nor depth, nor any other creature, shall be able to separate us from the love of God, which is in Christ Jesus our Lord.*
> *–Romans 8:35-39* (KJV)

Read in context with the rest of Romans chapter 8, the reader can clearly see Paul is addressing Christians here and referring to the special relationship God has with those who love Him. God has an unconditional love for the unregenerate as one can see in John 3:16, which tells us that for the love of the whole world God gave His only begotten Son in order to provide a way of salvation to all of mankind. Likewise, the account of the rich young ruler in Mark 10:21-22 says Jesus "beholding him loved him," even though Jesus knew the young man loved his wealth and possessions more than Jesus and would reject His offer to be His disciple. Jesus loved him although the young man went away lost and still in his sins; but just because Jesus loved the man doesn't mean he was saved.

Paul spoke accurately when he wrote in this passage that nothing can separate us from the **love** of Christ. No power on earth or in the heavens above or in the depths of hell can change the fact of God's love for us. Even our own rejection of Him cannot change His love. **Notice, though, he did *not* write that our own willful rebellion cannot separate us from the *salvation* of Christ.** God in His great compassion clearly extends a general love to all of mankind, but **there is a more intimate, conditional love** expressed in John 14:21 by Jesus:

> **Whoever has my commands and obeys them, he is the one who loves me. He who loves me will be loved by my Father, and I too will love him and manifest myself to him.**

Take note of Jesus' unambiguous words: *He who has my commands and keeps them...will be loved by my Father, and I too will love him.* The obvious inference is that living a life characterized by sin and rebellion is *not* keeping Christ's commands, and rebellious sinners are not in the love of God – not the special kind of love that God reserves for His own.

So then, can anyone or anything separate the true Christian from the **salvation** of God? Suffice it to say, no source outside our own wills can take away the special kind of love God has for those who love Him, and therefore no force outside our own wills can take away our salvation. Therefore, it is not valid to read the doctrine of eternal security into these verses, since the conditionality of God's love is asserted throughout the whole of Scripture. The entire listing of forces Paul mentions in Romans 8:35-36 – death, life, angels, principalities, powers, etc. – are all elements outside the moral choice of the believer. Even Paul's reference to "any other creature" suggests *other creatures* are beings other than believers. Therefore, an eternal security doctrine would demand we interpret Romans 8:38-39 to mean neither death nor life, neither angels nor demons, neither the present nor the future, nor any other powers, NOR ANY WILLFUL OR UNREPENTED DISOBEDIENCE AND REBELLION can separate us from the SALVATION of God.

Clearly, this is not what Romans 8:38-39 is communicating. God's love and His salvation are two very different things. And true belief – *pisteuo* – is characterized by our own moral choices expressed by a *continual clinging* to our Object of worship.

Tenet #2
**"God Himself will secure one's salvation even
in spite of one's beliefs or lifestyle"**

*Being confident of this very thing, that He which
began a good work in you will perform it until the
day of Jesus Christ.*
–Philippians 1:6

This verse has become one of the pillars of the eternal security doctrine. However, to get eternal security out of this verse is to read it with eternal security in mind in the first place. This verse is lifted out of a passage which, in its entirety, suggests Paul is communicating something other than an unconditional eternal security of the Christians in Philippi. Let us read the verse in context with the rest of the passage:

> *³I thank my God every time I remember you. ⁴In all my prayers for all of you, I always pray with joy ⁵because of your partnership in the gospel from the first day until now, ⁶being confident of this, that He who began a good work in you will perform it until the day of Jesus Christ. ⁷It is right for me to feel this way about all of you, since I have you in my heart; for whether I am in chains or defending and confirming the gospel, all of you share in God's grace with me.*
> *–Philippians 1:3-7*

Paul had the utmost confidence in the Philippian Christians, because they had shared in actively supporting his ministry. Even in Paul's imprisonment, they willingly identified themselves with him by sending a member of their congregation to visit him and by providing financial gifts. Paul stated clearly that because they had partnered with him "from the first day until now," he had confidence they would continue to persevere and God's sanctifying work would be made complete in them. Nowhere does this passage state that Paul's confidence was in an unconditional eternal security. Rather, **he said his confidence was based upon their past faithfulness in partnering financially with him in his ministry.**

Look again at verse 6. What is it Paul said God would complete? He said God would complete the "good work" he began in them. So, what is the *good work* Paul is referring to? The text is very plain. Paul is referring to their generous financial support of his ministry. Paul simply states that the Philippians' past record of support gave him confidence that God would continue to perfect them in the ministry of giving. Bear in mind, Paul was addressing his statements to a church and commenting on their corporate ministry. What he did *not* say was that God would complete His good work of *salvation* in each and every individual regardless of their conduct. This simple truth becomes obvious when taking an unbiased look at the Scriptures and considering context.

Tenet #3
"No one who comes to Christ shall be lost"

And this is the Father's will Who hath sent me, that all of which He hath given me I should lose nothing, but should raise it up again on the last day.
–John 6:39 (KJV)

There is a stark difference between a *decree* of God – something that will not change – and the *permissive will* of God, or, in other words, His desire. Second Peter 3:9 says it is God's *will* that no one would perish, but *everyone* would come to repentance. Obviously, however, this is not what happens. Not everyone comes to repentance. Endless multitudes are occupying hell this very moment, and yet the Scriptures say this it is not God's will (desire) that they be there. In fact, the word translated into English as *will* in this verse is the Greek word *theléma*, which means *a preference or desire*, and implies a *desire*, a *wish*, or *pleasure*. So, John 6:39 could be accurately translated this way: *This is the Father's **preference**...*

However, in keeping with our rule to interpret Scripture in light of Scripture, let us read the entire passage in which this verse appears.

> *35Then Jesus declared, "I am the bread of life. He who comes to me will never go hungry, and he who believes in me will never be thirsty. 36But as I told you, you have seen me and still you do not believe. 37All that the Father gives me will come to me, and whoever comes to me I will never drive away. 38For I have come down from heaven not to do my will but to do the will of Him who sent me. 39And this is the Father's will who has sent me, that I shall lose none of all that He has given me, but raise them up at the last day. 40For my Father's will is that everyone who looks to the Son and believes in Him shall have eternal life, and I will raise him up at the last day."*
> *-John 6:35-40*

The context of these verses has nothing to do with unconditional eternal security. The first observation we can make in that regard is found in verse 37, where Jesus states he will not *drive away* those who come to him. He did not say we couldn't walk away on our own, as many of His disciples did after He finished His dissertation at the end of this chapter in verse 66: *From this time many of His disciples turned back and no longer followed Him,* thus proving again that verse 39 was not speaking of unconditional eternal security.

We see another clue of this truth in verse 40, where Jesus says, *For my Father's will is that everyone who looks to the Son and believes [pisteuo] in Him shall have eternal life.* Again, *pisteuo* means a *continual clinging and adhering to.* In a very literal sense, Jesus is saying that everyone who *clings to Him as their only hope of salvation and adheres to His commandments as a lifestyle* shall have eternal life. Nowhere does John 6:39 imply that those who persevere for a little while and then abandon the faith or begin living in willful rebellion against God's commandments will have eternal life.

Tenet #4
"Our inheritance is guaranteed, no matter what"

> *13And you also were included in Christ when you heard the word of truth, the gospel of your salvation. Having believed* [pisteuo], *you were marked in him with a seal, the promised Holy Spirit, 14who is a deposit guaranteeing our inheritance until the redemption of those who are God's possession – to the praise of His glory.*
> *-Ephesians 1:13-14*

The fact that this verse uses the present active participle *pisteuo* is enough to overturn the argument of this being an eternal security verse. Only those who persevere by continually clinging to the Savior *(pisteuo)* are the ones the Holy Spirit marks with a seal guaranteeing our salvation. Notice the verse does not say believers can't ever break or remove this seal themselves. The whole of Scripture proves we can.

Observe also that the Holy Spirit is only a *deposit* or a down payment on our inheritance and **we do not possess the inheritance in its fullness until the day of our redemption. The full consummation of this promise is made only to** *those who endure to the end* **(Matthew 10:22).** The Lord preserves the *faithful* (Psalm 31:23), and those who are *faithful until death* will receive a crown of life (Revelation 3:5, 21).

Tenet #5
"No one is able to remove a person from his/her salvation; nor can someone remove themselves"

> *27My sheep hear my voice, and I know them, and they follow me: 28And I give unto them eternal life; and they shall never perish, neither shall any man pluck them out of my hand. 29My Father, which gave*

> *them to me, is greater than all; and no man is able*
> *to pluck them out of my Father's hand.*
> *–John 10:27-29 (KJV)*

The original Greek renders the words *hear* and *follow* in the present tense. In other words, the text might more accurately be rendered as *My sheep are **hearing** my voice…and they are **following** me.* This implies that only those who are hearing and following Christ presently are His sheep. Those who are living in continual and unrepentant sin are not the sheep of Christ, because they are neither hearing nor following Him.

Notice also the text says, *no **man** is able to **pluck** them out of My hand.* The meaning is clear. **Pluck implies a taking away by force against one's will. Man implies someone other than the sheep themselves,** whether that be the devil, demons, or other people – forces outside of God and the believer. No one is able to take a Christian by force away from Jesus against his/her will. The text does *not* say, however, that sheep can't decide to go their own way and stop following the Shepherd. Followers of Christ cannot be removed from their secure position against their will, but deserters of the faith and those who live in willful and unrepentant rebellion *remove themselves* from the promises of security.

What people, then, are secure in their salvation? The sheep who are presently hearing and following. "But is this not salvation by works?" eternal security proponents might ask. Not at all. It is consistent with *pisteuo* faith as communicated in John 3:16 and James 2:15-26.

Tenet #6
"People who leave the church and the faith were never saved in the first place"

> *They went out from us, but they did not really*
> *belong to us. For if they had belonged to us, they*

> *would have remained with us; but their going*
> *showed that none of them belonged to us.*
> *-1 John 2:19*

This verse has been used to support the idea that if someone in the church leaves the faith, it proves he or she was never saved to begin with. However, if this verse truly supports the concept of an unconditional eternal security, then we could *never* know if those who labor alongside us in our churches for the sake of the gospel are truly saved or just *professing* Christians who might not be saved at all. Yet this is contradictory to what the Bible teaches. The Scriptures say in numerous places, *by their fruit you will recognize them.* Furthermore, Revelation 22:18-19 is just one of many verses showing how genuine believers can forfeit their salvation:

> ¹⁸*I warn everyone who hears the words of the prophecy of this book: If anyone adds anything to them, God will add to him the plagues described in this book.* ¹⁹*And if anyone takes words away from this book of prophecy, GOD WILL TAKE AWAY FROM HIM HIS SHARE IN THE TREE OF LIFE AND IN THE HOLY CITY, which are described in this book.*

Likewise, if the unconditional eternal security interpretation of 1 John 2:19 is correct, we would have to reject at least a dozen other Biblical examples of people who were genuine believers and then turned away from Christ to their ultimate spiritual destruction. King Saul, for example, was undoubtedly a true believer who once laid on the ground and prophesied for hours (see 1 Samuel 19:23-24). It says the Spirit of the Lord came upon King Saul, and he prophesied along with other prophets in the presence of Samuel. A person can't prophesy in this way and not be saved. Yet King Saul drifted from God and later became a murderous madman who died in his sin.

Consider also the dozens of disciples previously mentioned in John 6:66 who deserted Jesus. They, along with King Saul, provide just a couple of examples of people who were once saved and later turned from the ways of God, never to return.

One other such example is King Solomon. It can be safely stated that Solomon was indeed once a fully devoted follower of Jehovah early in his life. God once appeared to him in a dream and told him to ask for anything, and God was very pleased when Solomon asked for wisdom. In response, God greatly blessed Solomon. But Solomon later in his life did exactly what God told him not to do, which was to marry foreign women. Solomon disobeyed and, as a result, he began worshipping the foreign gods of his pagan wives and even built altars and edifices for them! Solomon was committing high treason against the God of the Universe, a total disregard of the first of the Ten Commandments: *You shall have no other gods before Me*, and *You shall not make unto yourselves a graven image*. Idol worship is treason against God in the highest order, and according to 1 Corinthians 6:9-10 and Galatians 5:20-21, no idolater will enter the Kingdom of heaven. (If you're wondering, many believe King Solomon to be the author of the book of Ecclesiastes. If so, his writings may indicate his repentant heart later in life).

Moving on from the Old Testament, there is the case of Hymenaeus and Philetus, two men mentioned by Paul in his second letter to Timothy. Paul condemned these men for "wandering away from the truth" (2 Timothy 2:18). The implication of Paul's condemnation is that these two men were once true followers of Christ who were devoted members of the church but who then "wandered away from the truth" to follow and teach a false and damning doctrine.

Another who wandered from the truth was Demas, a believer numbered among the early apostles. He was a trusted ministry companion of Paul, mentioned first in Colossians 4:14 when Paul sent Demas' greetings to the Colossian Christians along with those of Luke. In a later letter to Timothy, Paul denounced Demas for having deserted him because Demas "loved this world" (2 Timothy 4:10).

The apostle John wrote in 1 John 2:15 that if anyone loves the world, the love of the Father is not in him, and James 4:4 reads:

> *You adulterous people, don't you know that friendship with the world is hatred toward God? Anyone who chooses to be a friend of the world becomes an enemy of God.*

Demas began by running a good race. He was apparently a devoted Christian and a committed laborer in the Church. However, he was led astray by his attraction to the world. Instead of finishing the course, he left behind the legacy of a deserter. Unless he later repented, which we have no record of, Demas did not inherit eternal life in heaven, because, as James says, his love of the world made him an enemy of God.

The truth of the conditional offer of salvation is perhaps no more obvious than in Jesus' parable of the unmerciful servant in Matthew 18. Jesus used the parable to illustrate the kingdom of heaven. He explained how a king called in a particular servant who owed him such an extraordinary amount of money that the servant would never be able to pay it back. Begging more time in which to pay back the debt, the servant fell to his knees in desperation before the monarch. The king, seeing the servant's brokenness, had compassion on him and forgave the entire amount. However, this same servant then went out and demanded from a fellow servant payment in full of a comparatively meager debt owed him. He even went so far as to have the fellow servant thrown into prison. When the king heard about this, he was furious. He called in the servant and said:

> [32]*"You wicked servant," he said. "I cancelled all that debt of yours because you begged me to.*

> *³³Shouldn't you have had mercy on your fellow servant just as I had on you?" ³⁴In anger his master turned him over to the jailers to be tortured, until he should pay back all he owed. ³⁵THIS IS HOW MY HEAVENLY FATHER WILL TREAT EACH OF YOU UNLESS YOU FORGIVE YOUR BROTHER FROM YOUR HEART.*
> *-Matthew 18:32-35*

Remember, Jesus used this parable to explain the kingdom of heaven (see Matthew 18:23). The servant who was forgiven is analogous to the Christian. It is the picture of someone who had a debt of sin too great to ever reconcile. However, just as God has done through Jesus, God has forgiven that debt for those who come to Him in repentance. Because we as Christians have been forgiven a debt too great to pay back, God expects us to show the same mercy toward those who have offended us. If we do not, but instead demand restitution by holding grudges and/or acting spitefully toward the offender, Jesus explains we can have our forgiveness revoked by God.

As the Confraternity of Christian Doctrine Bible Commentary concisely put it regarding Matthew 18:35: "The Father's forgiveness, already given, will be withdrawn at the final judgment for those who have not imitated His forgiveness by their own."

It could not be clearer that salvation is a *conditional* offer, as there are many examples of this in Scripture. In fact, **a careful examination of Scripture will show over a dozen other examples of people who were in the faith but later fell away.**

Once again, to understand any one verse we must consider the context in which it appears. Rather than isolating 1 John 2:19 and using it to suggest that people who fall away from the church were never saved to begin with, we must carefully consider the context. Here is how the entire passage reads where 1 John 2:19 appears:

¹⁵*Do not love the world or anything in the world.* **IF ANYONE LOVES THE WORLD, THE LOVE OF THE FATHER IS NOT IN HIM.** *¹⁶For everything in the world – the cravings of the sinful man, the lust of his eyes and the boasting of what he has and does – comes not from the Father but from the world. ¹⁷The world and its desires pass away,* **BUT THE MAN WHO DOES THE WILL OF GOD LIVES FOREVER.** *¹⁸Dear children, this is the last hour, and as you have heard that the antichrist is coming, even now many antichrists have come. This is how we know it is the last hour. ¹⁹They went out from among us, but they did not really belong to us. For if they had belonged to us, they would have remained with us; but their going showed that none of them belonged to us. ²⁰But you have an anointing from the Holy One, and all of you know the truth. ²¹I do not write to you because you do not know the truth, but because you do know it and because no lie comes from the truth. ²²Who is the liar? It is the man who denies that Jesus is the Christ. Such a man is an antichrist – he denies the Father and the Son. ²³No one who denies the Son has the Father; whoever acknowledges the Son has the Father also. ²⁴As for you,* **SEE THAT WHAT YOU HAVE HEARD FROM THE BEGINNING REMAINS IN YOU. IF IT DOES, YOU ALSO WILL REMAIN IN THE SON AND IN THE FATHER.** *²⁵And this is what He has promised us – even eternal life.* **I AM WRITING THESE THINGS TO YOU ABOUT THOSE WHO ARE TRYING TO LEAD YOU ASTRAY.** *As for you, the anointing you received from Him remains in you, and you do not need anyone to teach you. But as His anointing teaches you about all things and just as that anointing is real, not counterfeit – just as it has taught you,* **REMAIN IN HIM.** *²⁸And now, dear children,* **CONTINUE IN HIM,**

> *SO THAT WHEN HE APPEARS WE MAY BE CONFIDENT*
> *AND UNASHAMED BEFORE HIM AT HIS COMING. ²⁹IF*
> *YOU KNOW THAT HE IS RIGHTEOUS, YOU KNOW*
> *THAT EVERYONE WHO DOES WHAT IS RIGHT HAS*
> *BEEN BORN OF HIM.*
> *-1 John 2:15-29*

Contrary to the notion of verse 19 teaching that those who do not remain in the church were never really saved to begin with, we can clearly see from the entire context that this is not even what the passage is about. John begins this passage by warning his readers to not love the world or else the love of the Father would not reside in them – a very *anti* eternal security statement.

John then warns his readers about the many heretics of the time. Church history tells us the antichrists John is referring to in this passage were the early Gnostics, who held particular sway in encroaching upon the minds of some believers. Gnostics taught that sin dwelt in the body only, making the body totally evil at the exclusion of the spirit, which was totally good. **According to the Gnostic philosophy, therefore, an individual could live in wickedness in the body while simultaneously living pure and holy in the spirit, which sounds a lot like how some people use the doctrine of eternal security to justify living in willful sin. Is the eternal security doctrine a leftover fragment of Gnosticism?** I think we could make the case that it is. John set out in this letter to refute the evil of this heresy and calls the ones who perpetuate it *antichrists.*

John then clearly states his purpose for bringing these things to the attention of his readers in verse 26 of First John 2: *I am writing these things to you about those who are trying to lead you astray.* He was hoping to keep his readers from being seduced by a false gospel that allows for continual self-indulgence and wickedness, and he therefore continues re-instilling what his readers undoubtedly already knew – which was to *remain in Him* and *continue in Him* so they would *remain in the Father and in the*

Son. He clearly states a condition for remaining in the Father and in the Son, and the condition was that they remain in Him.

If it was not possible for these early Christians to be seduced by a false gospel of unrestrained and unholy living, and therefore to fall away, what value would these warnings be to his readers? If it was not possible for Christians to be deceived and fall away to eternal damnation, then Peter and Paul would have never offered these sorts of sober warnings.

It could not be more clear that 1 John 2:19 is *not* an eternal security verse. To the contrary, it is part of a very *anti* eternal security passage.

In order to shed additional light on this belief that those who leave the church or turn away to engage in wickedness were "never saved to begin with," consider 1 Timothy 5:14, 15, which reads:

> ¹⁴*So I counsel younger widows to marry, to have children, to manage their homes and to give the enemy no opportunity for slander.* ¹⁵*Some have in fact already* **TURNED AWAY** *to follow Satan.*

The inference of this verse is obvious: One cannot *turn away to follow Satan* unless he or she was first following someone else. Since there is only one other possibility as to whom else these widows were following prior to their turning away to follow Satan, the widows to whom Paul is speaking were obviously followers of Jesus. Furthermore, verse 11 clearly states that these widows had a "dedication to Christ." We can come to no other conclusion except that Paul is referring to widows who were once followers of Christ who then turned away and followed Satan, probably by plunging into sexual immorality and/or into gossip, meddling or idleness (see verse 13 of 1 Timothy 5).

Why did these widows turn away to follow Satan? Verses 11 through 13 tell us the reason:

> ¹¹**As for younger widows, do not put them on such a list** [of widows in the church]**. For WHEN THEIR SENSUAL DESIRES OVERCOME THEIR DEDICATION TO CHRIST, they want to marry.** ¹²**Thus they bring judgment on themselves, because THEY HAVE BROKEN THEIR FIRST PLEDGE.** ¹³**Besides, they get into the habit of being idle and going about from house to house. And not only do they become idlers, but also busybodies who talk nonsense, saying things they ought not to.**

Paul states the sensual desires of the younger widows in the church overcome their dedication to Christ, and as a result, they want to break the vow previously made to be a widow dedicated to Christ and, instead, once again marry. He warns that the breaking of this vow brings judgment, so it's better to not make a vow at all. This is why he counseled the younger widows to not make such a vow but rather to remarry if they so desired, and the church leaders should not put them on a list of financial support like the older widows for that reason. This advice would also help prevent the younger widows from sinning further by being idle, gossiping meddlers. Paul makes the point here that judgment awaits those who once made a vow to Christ only to break it and then career off into sinful living.

Tenet #7
"A Christian's inheritance can never perish, even if he/she abandons it"

> ³**Praise be to the God and Father of our Lord Jesus Christ! In His great mercy He has given us new birth into a living hope through the resurrection of Jesus Christ from the dead,** ⁴**and into an inheritance that can never perish, spoil or fade – kept in heaven for you.**
> **-1 Peter 1:3, 4**

As with the other Scriptures we have examined so far, those who use 1 Peter 1:3-4 to support an eternal security doctrine have inadvertently – or perhaps intentionally in some cases – failed to consider the context. If you read on in verse 5, you see once again a *condition* attached to the inheritance that can never perish. It says, **who through faith** *are shielded by God's power until the coming of the salvation...*

What is faith? The word translated into English as *faith* in this verse is the Greek word *pistis* (pist-is), the most literal translation of which is *to persuade*. The Greek understanding of this word is not limited to our narrow use of the English word *persuasion*, because the Greek language was very descriptive, and words had different meanings depending on their use and context. According the Strong's Exhaustive Concordance of the Bible, *pistis* as it is used here implies *conviction, constancy, and fidelity.* In other words, the kind of faith resulting in a salvation that will never perish is characterized by a constant conviction that Christ is the only hope of redemption demonstrated in obedience to His commands (fidelity). This is yet another example of the *pisteuo* kind of belief.

Tenet #8
"Everyone who comes to faith overcomes, even if they don't persevere"

⁴Everyone born of God overcomes the world. This is the victory that has overcome the world, even our faith. ⁵Who is it that overcomes the world? Only he who believes that Jesus is the Son of God.
-1 John 5:4, 5

With what we have learned already about the Greek language, this verse can be cleared up with only a small amount of explanation. The word *faith* in verse 4 is the same word we examined in 1 Peter 3. It is the Greek word *pistis*, which once again implies a constancy of belief, demonstrated in fidelity. Likewise, the word *believes* in verse 5 is the Greek word *pisteuo*, which means a constant adherence and clinging to.

These Greek words magnify the meaning of this verse and make it very plain. What is the victory that overcomes the world? It is a faith in Christ resulting in a changed life – one marked by repentance and adherence to His commands. Who is it who overcomes the world? Only he who adheres to Christ until the end of his life will overcome.

And what about the context? Verses 3 and 18 of this same passage shed more light upon its meaning. They read: ***This is love for Christ: to obey His commands... We know that anyone born of God does not continue to sin.*** If we love Christ, we will obey His commands. If we ever stop obeying His commands, it means we have stopped loving Him. If we stop loving Him, we will not inherit eternal life.

This truth flies in the face of the concept of a person being able to live in blatant rebellion against God's commands and still be called a child of God. According to Scripture the person who lives in blatant rebellion against God's commands can no longer be called a child of God. A person cannot be saved and under grace who chooses to live his life as a practicing homosexual, an adulterer, a thief, a liar, an occultist, or an atheist.

Tenet #9
"God will prevent you from falling away"

To Him Who is able to keep you from falling and to present you before His glorious presence without fault...
-Jude 24

The Greek word translated into English as "falling" in this verse is the negative participle *aptaistlos* (ap-tah-ee-stos), which implies to *not stumble*, or, according to the Strong's Concordance, *without sin.* If we isolate this verse from the rest of Scripture and read it as a stand-alone statement, we could just as easily conclude that after we become Christians, God will keep us from ever sinning again. Clearly, this is not what this verse is suggesting.

First of all, in keeping with our rule of scriptural context, we dare not isolate this verse from the rest of Jude's letter or the overarching message of the entire canon of Scripture.

Jude begins his letter with comments which seem very anti-eternal security:

> *³Dear friends, although I was very eager to write to you about the salvation we share, I felt I had to write and urge you to contend for the faith that was once for all entrusted to the saints. ⁴For certain men whose condemnation was written about long ago have secretly slipped in among you. They are godless men, who change the grace of our God into a license for immorality and deny Jesus Christ our only Sovereign and Lord.*
> (vv. 3-4)

As in our modern times, there were people in the early church who were perverting the gospel message and suggesting a person could live in unrestrained immorality and still be a Christian. Jude flatly refutes that claim. In fact, he says by doing so the Lord Jesus is denied.

So then, is Jude suggesting in verse 24 that when a person becomes a Christian, God will prevent him/her from falling away? Not at all. Jude 24 is simply agreeing with the Apostle Peter:

> *³His divine power has given us everything we need for life and godliness THROUGH OUR KNOWEDGE OF HIM who called us by His own glory and goodness. ⁴Through these He has given us His very great and precious promises, so that through*

them you may participate in the divine nature and escape the corruption in the world caused by evil desires. ⁵For this very reason, make every effort to add to your faith goodness; ⁶and to goodness, knowledge; and to knowledge, self-control; and to self-control, perseverance; and to perseverance, godliness; ⁷and to godliness, brotherly kindness; and to brotherly kindness, love. ⁸For if you possess these qualities in increasing measure, they will keep you from being ineffective and unproductive in your knowledge of our Lord Jesus Christ. ⁹But if anyone does not have them, he is nearsighted and blind, and has forgotten that he has been cleansed from his past sins. ¹⁰THERFORE, MY BROTHERS, BE ALL THE MORE EAGER TO MAKE YOUR CALLING AND ELECTION SURE. FOR IF YOU DO THESE THINGS, YOU WILL NEVER FALL...
        -2 Peter 1:3-10

There are two primary points to consider in these verses:

First, Peter clearly implies that the believers to whom he is writing *can* fall away. He didn't say they would never sin. He did say that as long as they appropriated the provisions God has made for our faith, those provisions would keep us from becoming ineffective in our faith. However, if they did not appropriate those provisions, then falling away was possible.

Secondly, these verses, as stated earlier, agree with Jude 24. God *is* able to keep us from falling, and He has made the provisions for every aspect of our faith through His Holy Spirit, through Scripture, through Biblical dissemination from godly teachers, and prayer. **As long as we practice these disciplines and appropriate His provisions, and as long as we cling to the Savior, we will never fall away,** because nothing and no one outside of our own wills can rip us from the grasp of our beloved Savior (Romans 8:38-39). We must understand, though, a believer *can choose to walk away* from the Savior's loving embrace, and he/she *can* fall away due to lack of discipline, as 2 Peter 1:3-10 clearly explains. God is not a dictator. He will honor our choices.

Clearly, the foundation upon which the eternal security doctrine is built is sinking sand. It cannot hold up under careful Biblical exegesis.

6

Eternal Security and Predestination

Any discussion on unconditional eternal security will eventually come around to the concept of predestination. Predestination and eternal security are tied together with a pretty short rope, and one of the verses used to support this idea is Romans 8:29, 30:

> [29]**For those God foreknew He also predestined to be conformed to the likeness of His Son, that He might be the firstborn among many brothers.** [30]**And those He predestined, He also called; those He called, He also justified; those He justified, He also glorified.**

A casual reading might lead one to believe this verse supports a predestination doctrine. A more careful and thorough reading, however, will show otherwise. Let's put this under the microscope.

The attempt to use this text to show God predestines certain people for salvation actually backfires, because the "foreknowledge" the Apostle Paul speaks of here is self-limiting if we read it through the lens of predestination. Paul says, "Those who God *foreknew* He predestined." If we read a predestination doctrine into this verse, we are forced to also believe there are those who God did not foreknow, since the text says it is those God foreknew that He predestined. This would imply that the ones who were not predestined were not foreknown by God, suggesting God's knowledge is limited.

The predestination this text speaks of is not *who* is chosen to be included or excluded in God's Kingdom, but *what will happen* to all who choose Christ as their Savior. All who receive Christ will eventually be conformed to His image, justified and glorified. God predestines the *outcome* of the choice to be in Christ or not, but He doesn't predestine the choice itself.

God lives outside of time and space. He sees the beginning from the end. While He does not force anyone to love and serve Him, He knows beforehand who will and who will not. And for those who He knows will, He has arranged that those be conformed to the likeness of Jesus.

Another verse sometimes used to support the idea of predestined salvation is Proverbs 139:16:

> **Your eyes saw my unformed body; all my days were written in Your book and ordained for me before one of them came to be.**

There is a growing consensus among Bible scholars that this verse is poorly translated into English from the ancient Hebrew. Without going into a lengthy explanation of how and why the more common English translations of this verse are problematic, perhaps it would be simpler to refer to the most recent translation of the Old Testament by the Jewish Publication Society called the *Tanakh*. The Tanakh translates Proverbs 139:15-16 as follows:

> **¹⁵My frame is not concealed from You when I was shaped in a hidden place, knit together in the**

> *recesses of the earth.* ¹⁶*Your eyes saw my unformed*
> *limbs; they were all recorded in Your book; in due*
> *time they were formed, to the very last one of them.*

Notice this more precise and accurate translation says it was the Psalmist's unformed body parts that were recorded in God's book, not all of the days of his life.

The intent of this passage is to convey God's creative power and watchfulness over our lives beginning at conception, not to teach predestination. This point comes into even clearer focus when we read the verses with the proper translation applied.

God sees each of us even as our bodies are being formed in the darkness of the womb (the "hidden place"). He saw the body parts yet unformed, watching as they grew and developed. And as verse 14 points out, we are "fearfully and wonderfully made," which anchors the passage with its primary objective to give praise to God for the infinite and mysterious wonder of His creation.

Note also David's concluding remarks in Psalm 139, asking God to examine his heart for "offensive ways," praying that God would guide him "in the way everlasting." Why would David ask such a thing if he knew his salvation was secured regardless of what he did? This request shows he saw his salvation as contingent upon continuing to walk out his faith in word and deed.

Other Problems with Predestination

God once said of King Saul:

> *"I greatly regret that I have set up Saul as king,*
> *for he has turned back from following Me, and has*
> *not performed My commandments."*
> *-1 Samuel 15:11*

If God had predetermined the outcome of Saul's life, this verse suggests He was working against Himself, because He put a man in place who would not perform His will. To the contrary, God chose a man and granted him free will to accept and perform His commands or reject them.

Jesus also taught that salvation was available to anyone who chose the way of life. Christ concluded His Sermon on the Mount with several examples calling for action on the part of his hearers (see Matthew 7:13-27), presenting the choice of two mutually exclusive paths: one broad and the other narrow. If we hope to find the way of eternal life, we must choose the narrow path.

Of course, it is critical we understand all must be saved by grace through faith in the sacrifice of Christ, the outcome of which leads to a life of self-discipline and obedience.

The message of the Bible is that mankind has freedom of choice and we will be judged "according to our works" (Deuteronomy 30:19-20; Ecclesiastes 12:13-14; Acts 17:30-31; Revelation 20:13). While we are not saved by our works, nevertheless, our salvation expresses itself in corresponding fruitfulness.

Let's look at a passage deserving a second look. Pay close attention to Jesus' words:

> *⁶Then Jesus told this parable: "A man had a fig tree that was planted in his vineyard. He went to look for fruit on it, but did not find any. ⁷So he said to the keeper of the vineyard, 'Look, for the past three years I have come to search for fruit on this fig tree and haven't found any. Therefore cut it down! Why should it use up the soil?' ⁸'Sir,' the man replied, 'leave it alone again this year, until I dig around it and fertilize it. ⁹If it bears fruit next year, fine. But if not, you can cut it down.'"*
> *-Luke 13:6-8*

Bondage of the Will

One issue eternal security advocates use to support their doctrine is the concept of "bondage of the will," referring to the notion that none of us really have free will because God is sovereign and has planned everything ahead of time and knows the future. One example used to support this idea is Romans 9 where it says God hardened the heart of Pharaoh.

Many wise and reputable Bible commentators propose that when the Bible says God hardened Pharaoh's heart, what it really means is God simply facilitated a process which Pharaoh himself initiated. After all, the Bible repeatedly also states that Pharaoh hardened *his own* heart (see Exodus 8:15 and 32).

Dr. Norman Geisler, for instance, a highly-respected Bible scholar, suggests that God did not *directly* harden Pharaoh›s heart (or anyone else›s heart for that matter) contrary to their own free will, but only *indirectly*, through their own choices and actions. In a book he co-authored called *When Critics Ask*, Geisler and Howe say:

> God in His omniscience foreknew exactly how Pharaoh would respond, and He used it to accomplish His purposes. God ordained the means of Pharaoh's free but stubborn action...

And this is the position of many other respected commentators, but certainly not all. Some do suggest God directly and purposefully hardened Pharaoh's heart. But God is God, and He can do anything. For the person of faith, therefore, it's not a stretch to believe that in His foreknowledge God already knew what was in Pharaoh's heart, and He simply directed the hardness of heart already there to accomplish His own purposes.

This is a big topic because it also extends to people like Judas Iscariot, who betrayed Jesus. The Savior had to be betrayed in order to go to the cross and accomplish His mission of redemption. Was it therefore God Who ordained Judas to betray Jesus and go to hell? Well, no. *Somebody* was going to betray Jesus; that was God's unalterable will. But the betrayer didn't *have* to be Judas. Judas could have seen where his actions and motives were leading and chosen to abandon that course, and then somebody else would have eventually betrayed Jesus. Even after Judas betrayed Jesus, he also had ample opportunity to repent and make it right. But he didn't. And that was *his* choice, not God's.

God's sovereignty does not mean He pre-programs everyone and everything just as they happen. If that were true, we would have to arrive at some very troubling conclusions about the nature of God. When a little child is raped and murdered by a twisted, psychotic madman, for example, it was God who made the man that way and chose that particular child to suffer at his hands, according to this view. How can you love and trust a god who would ordain such a thing?

No one who opposes the idea of unconditional eternal security claims God is not sovereign. *Of course God is sovereign.* But we do disagree with how some camps understand and use this term. God is sovereign in the sense that He is first in order and rank; all-powerful, all-knowing, and omni-present. We are not suggesting God is not all-powerful. However, some doctrinal camps teach God's sovereignty removes the free will of man because He has pre-ordained every action, every decision, and every event, even horrendous evil. If we take the Calvinistic version of God's sovereignty to its ultimate and logical conclusion, we are forced to acknowledge it is God Himself ordaining and pre-planning genocidal events such as the annihilation of millions of Jews, Christians, and the undesirables of society by Adolph Hitler's Third Reich in Nazi Germany during World War II. While they may not have stopped to think about the far-reaching implications of their doctrine, the Calvinistic view of God forces a version of Him that makes Him out to be the author of rape, murder, torture, child abduction, slavery, racism, idolatry, bestiality, and every other vile evil imaginable. No, friends, God is not the author of evil. Rather, His Word declares, **every good and perfect gift is from above,** *coming down from the Father of the heavenly lights, who does not change like shifting shadows (James 1:17).* Murder, rape, and torture are works of Satan, not a loving God.

The fact that God is sovereign (first in order, power, and rank) does not mean our wills are "bound" in the sense we have no ability to truly decide for ourselves who and what to serve. *In the context of God's omniscience, He has ordained that mankind would have a free will in which to choose.*

God's Word is overflowing with passages about man's free will. From the very beginning, Adam and Eve were given free wills in which to choose good or evil, and they chose to disobey the Lord. The rich young ruler who asked Jesus about the way of life was given a choice to make by the Lord Jesus, and he chose to walk away. The Israelites were time and again confronted with the choice to either serve the Lord or to reject Him. Deuteronomy 30:19 says:

> *Today I have given you the choice between life and death, between blessings and curses. I call on heaven and earth to witness the choice you make. Oh, that you would choose life, that you and your descendants might live.*

Yes, God knows the beginning and the end. He has known the days of man even before the earth was made; and yet, mysteriously, in the context of His omniscience and sovereignty, He has given man a free will in which to choose and judges us according to those choices. Even when God clearly intervenes to turn the hearts of some people to Him even when they previously had no thought of Him, as He did with Saul on the road to Damascus, and even when it seems God may harden the hearts of others so they continue to rebel, as He did with Pharaoh, it is also true that God judges people according to their decisions and actions.

This is a great mystery that is impossible to understand this side of eternity by the limited thinking of the finite human mind. We must accept the fact that we see and understand as if looking through a darkened glass (see 1 Corinthians 13:12), and the ways of God are so much higher than ours that we will never be able to comprehend all the mysteries of His greatness (see Job 38-41).

The bottom line is that the idea of predestination does not support an unconditional eternal security doctrine because *conditional salvation,* free will, and a *form* of predestination all *co-exist* in God's Kingdom. We will never understand this fully, just as we will never understand how God can be one and yet exist in three distinct personalities: Father, Son, and Holy Spirit.

The predestination camp and the free will camp are *both* correct in the sense they both believe God is indeed sovereign. However, the free will camp believes that *in the context* of His sovereignty God has given man a free will and judges us accordingly, while the predestination camp seems to deny the existence of free will.

Is it really so much of a stretch to suggest that God has foreknowledge of each person's life, has laid before each of us a free will, and presented us with a *conditional* offer of salvation?

7

"Limited Atonement": Did Jesus Die only for Certain People?

An eternal security doctrine, which is based heavily on the Calvinistic interpretation of predestination, demands we view Christ's sacrifice on the cross as restricted to only a certain group of pre-selected people, thus the term, "Limited Atonement."

In his article describing the five points of Calvinism, Rev. Barry Gritters writes:

> Before any man or woman is born — in fact, before the world was made — God decided who would go to heaven and who would not. Before they did good or bad, God chose some to be His people and rejected others.

This particular point describes what Calvinists call Unconditional Election, one of the five points of Calvinism.

It occurred to me recently after listening to Bill Weise, author of *23 Minutes in Hell*, that if God decided before the world was made who would go to hell and who would go to heaven, and predestined each person for one of those two destinations, then God must be a very twisted and sick entity to preordain anyone for a place as horrific as hell. Bill Weise's vision provides grim detail of the horrors of hell, and it is impossible to reconcile the grace and mercy of God with the Calvinistic picture of God preordaining people to go to that place before they had even been born.

For the sake of revealing the Scriptural truth about the concept of unconditional election, however, let's dissect this.

Who are the "Elect?"

Unconditional Election is based partly on Matthew 11:27.

> *No one knows the Son except the Father, and no one knows the Father except the Son and anyone to whom the Son desires to reveal Him.*

Those who seek to uphold the doctrine of Unconditional Election believe they see substantiation in this statement of only certain people being granted a saving knowledge of God, the implication of which is that those who receive special revelation about God are elect, while everyone else is irreversibly damned.

Notice, however, there is nothing in this statement which suggests the ones to whom the Son reveals the Father is an exclusive group of people. Instead, the people to whom Jesus reveals the Father appear to be the same ones Jesus mentions in His very next statement: *"Come to me, all who labor and are heavy laden"* (Matthew 11:28). To whom is this invitation addressed? Everyone. Jesus used the word *all.* Although not everyone chooses to accept the special revelation of God in Christ Jesus, it is available to "all."

Jesus is simply describing the intimate communion He shares with the Father in His statement in Matthew 11:27. The word *know,* which Jesus uses twice in this statement, is the Greek word *epiginóskó,* which implies a knowledge based on personal experience. Jesus goes on to say that He shares this communion with whomever He wills. To whom, then, does Jesus reveal the Father? To "all" who come to Him and take His yoke up themselves.

Matthew 11:27, as many Bible scholars point out, is a call to discipleship. Jesus is saying that He welcomes anyone who wishes to become His disciple and will reveal the Father so they, too, can share in the special friendship which Jesus has with the Father.

In keeping with our rule to interpret the Bible with the Bible and refrain from reading anything in isolation, let's also consider 1 John 1:3.

> **We proclaim to you what we have seen and heard, so that you also may have fellowship with us. And our fellowship is with the Father and with his Son, Jesus Christ.**

What Jesus is saying in Matthew 11:27 is practically identical to what John writes here.

John writes that his fellowship is with the Father and with Jesus. Jesus, likewise, said His fellowship is with the Father.

John says his epistle is an invitation to other believers to share in this fellowship. Jesus, likewise, invites others to share in the fellowship He has with the Father.

Thus, Matthew 11:27 is an invitation to discipleship and intimate fellowship with the Father. This special relationship that Jesus speaks of here is not something that leads one to new life in Christ, but rather is a *result* of the New Birth. This revelation of God through Christ is an invitation to enter into deeper fellowship and relationship with the Father.

Let's go a step further and read the context in which Matthew 11:27 appears.

In verses 10 through 25 of Matthew 11, Jesus specifies that revelation about Him is granted to little children (or "babes" in some translations) but is hidden from the learned (v. 25). This is not because God has withheld Himself from intellectuals or hidden the revelation of Himself from them, but because many highly intelligent people tend to rely only on their own understanding and discard what is revealed by the Spirit. Those who are wise in their own eyes – the prideful – often depend upon their own powers of reason and reject the deeper revelations about God that must be accepted by faith. Those who are "babes" – the humble – understand their lowly state and are willing to seek and accept what the Spirit discloses about God and His Kingdom.

It may very well be, in fact, that the "wise" could also refer to the already-converted who think they have all the answers about God. I like what Jeremy Myers said in his article "Jesus Invites You into His Inner Circle of Friends" featured on RedeemingGod.com:

> *There is nothing in the context [of Matthew 11:25] to say that the "wise" could not be genuine believers who think they have God all figured out. There are countless numbers of Christians who have believed in Jesus for eternal life, but who refuse to enter into deeper fellowship with God because they refuse to believe what Jesus reveals to them about God.*

It seems as though many people prefer a strictly intellectual approach to their relationship with Jesus rather than a Spirit-led approach.

So then, this revelation of God in Jesus Christ spoken of in Matthew 11:27 is not referring to Jesus pre-ordaining some people to receive eternal life while rejecting others.

As a further point to ponder, consider that prior to the coming of Christ few people really understood what God was like. In fact, even great patriarchs of the faith like Moses who had great revelation didn't know God to the extent Jesus would reveal. Jesus made God known to mankind in a new way. To once again quote Jeremy Myers, "In Jesus, we have the fullest and most complete revelation of God's character that exists." Amen!

More Problems with Limited Atonement

Limited Atonement asserts that Jesus did not die for the sins of the whole world, just certain people. Referring again to Rev. Gritter's article:

> *Some teach that Christ made it possible for all men to be saved. But the questions that must be asked are: "If Christ died for all men, why are not all men saved?" "'Cannot God do what He desires to do?" "Is there something defective in Christ's death?" "Must man desire to be saved first?" But a man who is totally depraved cannot will to be saved. He hates God and wants nothing to do with Christ's death. So it must not be said that Christ died for all men.*

I'll be honest and admit that these words almost make my mouth hang open in disbelief. How can anyone who has read the Bible say Jesus did not die for everyone when God's Word specifically says He did? But eternal security advocates are forced with this outcome, because they claim people cannot lose a salvation for which they were predestined. And if only certain people were predestined to be saved and others predestined for damnation, then they are forced to conclude that Jesus died for only certain people.

Let's first deal with the comment in this quote about whether or not a depraved person can choose to be saved. Reverend Gritter and other Calvinists say this is impossible. But what does the Bible say? Let's take a second look at the Apostle Paul's statements in his letter to the Romans.

> **[18]The wrath of God is being revealed from heaven against all the godlessness and wickedness of men who suppress the truth by their wickedness. [19] For what may be known about God is plain to them, because God has made it plain to them. [20] For since**

> *the creation of the world God's invisible qualities, His*
> *eternal power and divine nature, have been clearly*
> *seen, being understood from His workmanship, so*
> *that men are without excuse.* *²¹For although they*
> *knew God, they neither glorified Him as God nor*
> *gave thanks to Him, but they became futile in their*
> *thinking and darkened in their foolish hearts.*
>   *-Romans 1:18-21*

To revisit a point in a previous chapter, the Bible teaches that sinful mankind already has an awareness of God built into us by God Himself because we are made in His image, and as this passage in Romans points out we can either choose to follow Him or choose to reject Him. So yes, depraved people can and do choose to respond to the God-knowledge already residing within us.

The assertion of Limited Atonement that Jesus' death did not apply to the sins of the whole world flies in the face of too many passages in the Bible to quote here, the most famous of which is John 3:16-17.

> *¹⁶For God so loved the* **WORLD** [that's everyone]
> *that He sent His only begotten Son that* **WHOSOEVER**
> [also referring to everyone] *would believe in Him*
> *should not perish but have everlasting life.* *¹⁷For God*
> *did not send His Son into the world to condemn the*
> *world, but in order that the world might be saved*
> *through Him.*

Obviously and clearly, God has in mind to extend the offer of salvation to the entire human population, to "whosoever" would respond.

Another clear passage refuting the idea that God only has in mind to save certain people and damn the rest, is 2 Peter 3:9.

The Lord is...not willing that ANY should perish,
but that ALL should come to repentance.

It is not God's preferred will that anyone would die and go to hell for all eternity. People go to hell only because God also has a *permissive* will, and He allows it to happen because He honors free will.

In God's Kingdom He has three expressions of His will:

1. **Decreed Will:** Events that will happen no matter what, such as the coming of the Messiah or Jesus being betrayed.
2. **Preferential Will:** God's preferences which sometimes happen and sometimes don't, such as His people walking in consistent obedience.
3. **Permissive Will:** Results of the Fall which displease God but He allows to happen, such as sin, sickness, and violence.

Regarding people going to hell, God has granted the grace of choice to each and every human being. Therefore, He has made provision to prevent that from happening for anyone who would respond to the free and all-inclusive offer of salvation. Jesus, a manifestation of God in flesh, came to earth to take upon Himself mankind's punishment for sin, so that *all* who place their faith in Him would be declared *not guilty* and redeemed from the curse of sin.

Reformed Theology, however, removes the need for any such redemptive sacrifice. If everyone is pre-programmed to respond to God or reject Him, and if all of our decisions and actions are already pre-arranged by God, thus removing the element of free will (another tenant of Calvinism), then a Scapegoat – a Savior – is unnecessary. *Jesus died for nothing if no one has the ability to choose for themselves anyway.*

Therefore, any theology that removes the need or even minimizes the importance of the death and resurrection of Jesus Christ is a false teaching, a heresy. The substitutional sacrifice of Jesus on the cross as the act of grace extending the offer of salvation to all of mankind is the preeminent doctrine upon which all of Christianity is based. Calvinism does not deny Jesus' death on the cross, but it certainly does remove the importance of it.

It defies both logic and Scripture to assume mankind has no ability to choose or reject God's offer of salvation. In fact, God once told the Israelites:

> *I call heaven and earth as witnesses today against you, that* I have set before *you life and death, blessing and cursing; therefore __CHOOSE__ life, that both you and your descendants may live.*
> *-Deuteronomy 30:19*

God likewise declared:

> *"But if serving the LORD seems undesirable to you, then __choose for yourselves__ this day whom you will serve, whether the gods your ancestors served beyond the Euphrates, or the gods of the Amorites, in whose land you are living. But as for me and my household, we will serve the LORD."*
> *-Joshua 24:15*

Clearly, God offers mankind a choice to serve Him or not serve Him. And if this were not true, we may as well throw out 99% of the Bible, along with the cross of Christ, because neither are needed for people whose choices are removed and whose destinies are pre-determined. No Biblical instruction is necessary for people whose free will is eradicated and whose choices are taken away. As such, an atoning sacrifice loses its splendor. **Amazing grace isn't really so amazing if Jesus died for people who are going to be saved anyway!**

The Bible *does* mention predestination, but these passages are wrongly interpreted by Calvinists to mean our lives and eternal destinies are beyond the realm of human choice. Rather, **these passages are not about who is destined to become a Christian, but about whom a Christian is destined to become.**

> ⁴*For He chose us in Him before the creation of the world to be holy and blameless in His sight. In love* ⁵*He predestined us for adoption to sonship through Jesus Christ, in accordance with the pleasure of His will.*
> -*Ephesians 1:4-5*

This passage is not suggesting God pre-programmed us to serve Him and, like robots, we have no choice in the matter. Rather, it is saying it was God's will that those who repent of their sins and turn to Christ will be declared holy and blameless by Christ's redeeming blood. This was His plan from the beginning. The predestination part is describing God's plan from eons ago regarding those responding to the free offer of salvation being adopted into His Kingdom as sons and daughters. It bears repeating then that *these passages are not about who is destined to become a Christian, but about whom a Christian is destined to become.*

There is a degree of healthy tension between the two camps of thinking since neither camp can fully understand the infinite and limitless nature of God. There is some degree of pre-arranged sovereignty with which we have to grapple, while at the same time acknowledging mankind's free will and God's resulting righteous judgement according to the choices we make.

Getting back to Limited Atonement, when a theological position is judged by the standards of the importance and splendor of the cross and what it accomplished, it is easier to spot heresy and false doctrine. False doctrine has been a problem since the beginning of Christianity, which is why the Apostle Peter wrote:

> *Therefore, dear friends, since you have been forewarned* [about false teachers]*, be on your guard so that you may not be carried away by the error of the lawless and <u>fall from your secure position</u>.*
> *-2 Peter 3:17*

"Fall from your secure position?" Wait. Christians can be secure in their salvation and then fall from that secure position? Yes. This is clearly what the Bible says.

The Scriptures teach that a person can accept and believe proper doctrine but then later be led astray if they are not watchful, thus "fall" away from their "secure position." It is of eternal importance what a person believes and practices. But thank God, He has given us a way to be reformed from deformed theology (false teaching) and turn from our sins and ignorance to embrace the true gospel of Jesus Christ, which is able to save your soul.

8

Making Sense of Romans 9

The doctrine of unconditional eternal security is built precariously upon the foundation of predestination, as we discussed in the previous chapter. Much of this belief comes from a surface reading of Romans 9. In other words, if one were to simply read through Romans 9 without a contextual understanding of what is being communicated by its author, the Apostle Paul, then predestination is perhaps a reasonable outcome. Therefore, let's examine Romans 9 more closely.

An Overview of a Fatalistic Interpretation of Romans 9

Some believe the ninth chapter of Romans demonstrates God's predetermined plan to save whomever He wishes and damn the rest. I'll refer to this belief as a *fatalistic* reading of Romans 9 throughout our discussion in this section. Fatalism refers to the idea that all events are predetermined and therefore inevitable and unchangeable.

The fatalistic interpretation may seem to have a strong case if one simply does a cursory reading of Romans 9. After all, didn't the Apostle Paul write that God has "mercy on whomever He wills, and He hardens whomever He wills" (vs. 18)? Paul then explains God's election by referring to God's choice of Isaac over Ishmael (9:7-8) and Jacob over Esau (9:10-13). Regarding Jacob and Esau, Paul writes:

> *[11]Yet before the twins were born or had done anything good or bad, in order that God's plan of election might stand, [12]not by works but by Him who calls, she was told, "The older will serve the younger. [13]So it is written: "Jacob I loved, but Esau I hated."*
> *-Romans 9:11-13*

God chose to "love" Jacob and "hate" Esau without regard to anything good or bad they had done because this love and hate was apparently determined before they were even born, according to the eternal security interpretation. Paul then concludes God's gift of salvation "does not depend on man's desire or effort, but on God's mercy" (Romans 9:16).

The fatalistic interpretation appears to be further supported as Paul goes on to illustrate God's relationship to mankind as similar to a potter and his lump of clay.

> *[21]Does not the potter have the right to make out of the same lump of clay some pottery for special purposes and some for common use? [22]What if God, although choosing to show His wrath and make His power known, bore with great patience the objects of His wrath—prepared for destruction? [23]What if He did this to make the riches of His glory known to the objects of His mercy, whom He prepared in advance for glory...*
> *-Romans 9:21-23*

The fatalistic interpretation of this passage sees God as simply creating some people for damnation in order to display His wrath and power while others He predetermines for salvation in order to display His mercy. According to this view, God has mercy on the latter but purposely hardens the hearts of the former so they cannot respond to His grace. And neither is based on any merits or evil God finds in the individual; it is based simply on God's predetermined choice. Paul's response, according to this view, is apparently to simply refute the legitimacy of the claim that predetermination seems unjust.

> *But who are you, a human being, to talk back to God? "Shall what is formed say to the one who formed it, 'Why did you make me like this?'"*
> *-Romans 9:20*

The case for the fatalistic reading of Romans 9 may initially look sound to those who do not understand the context. However, in examining this more closely in light of that context, we will see how Paul's discourse in Romans 9 is actually to establish a point which is in stark *contrast* to a fatalistic predetermination doctrine. Looking at this in relation to God's intentions, we will discover that God is not arbitrary, basing what He does on personal whims or random choice rather than reason or system. Rather, He is purposeful and even flexible in His dealings with mankind.

What Romans 9 is Actually Communicating

Many Bible scholars believe the doctrine of predetermined election unto salvation is read into the text by Calvinists and cannot be defended by an examination of the entire context of Romans chapters 9 through 11. Rather, Paul is describing the historical destiny of nations, not individuals. When the text refers to Isaac and Ishmael, it is referring to nations. Isaac grew up to be a figurehead of the nation of Israel, while Ishmael is a symbolic representation of pagan nations. This is likewise the case with Jacob and Esau.

For example, while discussing Romans 9:14-18, Roger Forster and Paul Marston in their book *God's Strategy in Human History* write, "The question at issue is not the eternal destiny of anyone, but the history of Israel and their significance as the chosen nation." This same understanding is expounded upon in a commentary on Romans 9:14-18 by Charles Cranfield:

> *It is important to stress that neither as they occur in Genesis nor as they are used by Paul do these words refer to the eternal destinies either of the two persons [Jacob and Esau] or of the individual members of the nations sprung from them; the reference is rather to the mutual relations of the two nations in history. What is here in question is not eschatological salvation or damnation, but the historical functions of those concerned and their relations to the development of the salvation history.*

In other words, Romans 9 is not talking about God predetermining certain individuals for salvation and others for damnation as a cursory reading might indicate. Rather, it is referring to God's election of nations in order to demonstrate His plan for salvation.

Paul launched this part of his discourse to the believers in Rome because some of the Jewish converts now saw a possible dichotomy in what was previously promised to the Jews and what was now unfolding with the Gentiles. While the fatalistic interpretation of Romans 9 assumes Paul concerned himself with individual salvation in this chapter, this is not the issue Paul was addressing. Paul's express purpose was to address whether or not "the Word of God had failed" (Romans 9:6). In other words, the question on the minds of some Jewish converts was apparently whether God's promise to be the God of the Jews and to preserve them as His covenant people had been revoked. The way in which Paul answered this concern further demonstrates his response was referring to God's relationship to nations, not with individual salvation. Paul effectively refuted the notion of God's covenant promises having failed by explaining how those promises were never based on nationality or outward obedience to the Old Testament Law in the first place. Rather, Paul showed how God had always applied His sovereign privilege to extend His grace to whatever nationality or people group He wanted, and did so, in fact, to the whole world.

The entire discourse in Romans 9 is intended to demonstrate the sovereign power of God in creating a people belonging to Himself who were formerly aliens of His grace. Paul states this very clearly when he wrote:

> **22What if God, although choosing to show His wrath and make His power known, bore with great patience the objects of his wrath—prepared for destruction? 23What if He did this to make the riches of His glory known to the objects of His mercy, whom He prepared in advance for glory— 24even us, whom He also called, not only from the Jews but also from the Gentiles? 25As He says in Hosea: "I will call them 'My people' who are not My people; and I will call her 'My loved one' who is not My loved one," 26and, "In the very place where it was said to them, 'You are not My people,' there they will be called 'children of the living God.' "**
> **-Romans 9:22-26**

This is where it gets fun!

Notice verse 22 mentions "the objects of His wrath – prepared for destruction." To whom is this referring? Gentiles! It is in reference to those who were apart from the covenant of Israel.

It goes on to say, "I will call them 'My people' who are not My people" (v. 25).

Obviously, the objects of God's wrath can later become objects of His mercy. Therefore, God can change His mind. God may determine to do something and then change course and do something different. Therefore, God's judgments are not fatalistic or unchangeable.

Are there other scriptural examples of this? Certainly.

In Exodus 32 we see where Moses bargained with God and influenced a change of heart. Yes, you read that correctly. A mere mortal influenced God to change His mind. Because of their idolatry, the LORD had determined to destroy the entire race of Israelites and spare only Moses.

> *⁹"I have seen these people," the Lord said to Moses, "and they are a stiff-necked people. ¹⁰Now leave Me alone so that My anger may burn against them and that I may destroy them. Then I will make you into a great nation."*

But Moses respectfully protested.

> *¹¹But Moses sought the favor of the Lord his God. "Lord," he said, "why should Your anger burn against Your people, whom You brought out of Egypt with great power and a mighty hand? ¹²Why should the Egyptians say, 'It was with evil intent that He brought them out, to kill them in the mountains and to wipe them off the face of the earth'? Turn from Your fierce anger; relent and do not bring disaster on Your people. ¹³Remember Your servants Abraham, Isaac and Israel, to whom You swore by Your own self: 'I will make your descendants as numerous as the stars in the sky and I will give your descendants all this land I promised them, and it will be their*

inheritance forever.' " ¹⁴**THEN THE LORD RELENTED**
and did not bring on His people the disaster He had
threatened.

There is a similar example in the book of Jonah where God had pronounced the death sentence to all the Ninevites on a specific, determined day. "Forty more days and Nineveh will be overturned," proclaimed Jonah on God's behalf (see Jonah 3:4). Yet God did not destroy them because they repented. The LORD God changed His mind.

> *When God saw their actions—that they had turned from their evil ways—He relented from the disaster He had threatened to bring upon them.*
> *-Jonah 3:10*

Jonah was actually displeased by God's mercy, however. He acknowledged God's nature, that He is prone to relenting, changing course from a previously-determined judgment.

> *¹Jonah, however, was greatly displeased, and became angry. ²So he prayed to the LORD, saying, "O LORD, is this not what I said while I was still in my own country? This is why I was so quick to flee toward Tarshish. I knew that You are a gracious and compassionate God, slow to anger, abounding in loving devotion—One who relents from sending disaster.*
> *-Jonah 4:1-2 (BSB)*

Getting back to Romans 9 we see an example of God making a similar pronouncement and then changing course. The Gentile pagans were the objects God's wrath and were "prepared for destruction" (Romans 9:22). Yet the very next verse refers to the same people as "objects of His mercy" (v. 23). Which is it?

It is *both*.

People who were once objects of God's wrath later became objects of His mercy. In other words, it was previously only the Jews who knew God's mercy, and Gentiles were "excluded from citizenship in Israel and foreigners to the covenants of the promise, without hope and without God in the world" (Ephesians 2:12). But now in Christ Jesus "you who once were far away have been brought near by the blood of Christ" (Ephesians 2:13).

Paul's discourse in Romans 9 is not to demonstrate predetermined and unchangeable election, but rather just the opposite. Paul is describing the Gospel in a nutshell, that salvation must be received by faith and not by works, which is why only a remnant of Israel shall be saved because of their reliance on works, whereas the Gentiles are now able to experience God's grace by faith. Pay attention to how Paul summarized his argument along these lines:

> [30]*What then shall we say? That the Gentiles, who did not pursue righteousness, have obtained it, a righteousness that is by faith;* [31]*but the people of Israel, who pursued the law as the way of righteousness, have not attained their goal.* [32]*Why not? Because they pursued it not by faith but as if it were by works. They stumbled over the stumbling stone.*
> *-Romans 9:30-32*

Paul begins his summary by asking, "What then shall we say" (vs. 30). If the fatalistic interpretation was accurate, we might expect Paul to conclude by saying something along the lines of God having predetermined who is elect and who is not, and that's unchangeable; and since He is the sovereign LORD, we don't have the right to object or question Him. But the great apostle says nothing of the sort. Rather, he summarizes his response to the concerns of the Jewish converts by explaining how the Gentiles who did not *strive* for righteousness (i.e. they didn't work for it) have attained it through faith, but Israel, who *did* strive for righteousness did not succeed because their goal was works-oriented righteousness based on the Law of Moses, which they ultimately failed at keeping anyway (vs. 30–32).

This is a very important point to consider. What God has always looked for in people is faith. The Jews did not "strive" for faith but rather chose to trust in their own self-righteousness. Many Gentiles, however, acknowledged the universal truth of mankind's reprehensible nature and simply believed God would justify them anyway based on faith in His grace through Jesus Christ.

This theme is weaved throughout chapters 9 through 11 of Romans. Paul explains in Romans 11:20 how the Jews "were broken off *because of their unbelief.*" This is why they were hardened (Romans 11:7, 25), while the Gentiles sought God by faith and were "grafted in" (11:23).

In an excellent article entitled "How Do You Respond to Romans 9," Greg Boyd writes:

> We see that God's process of hardening some and having mercy on others is not arbitrary: God expresses "severity toward those who have fallen [the nation of Israel] but kindness toward you [believers] provided you continue in His kindness" (11:22). **God has mercy on people and hardens people in response to their belief or unbelief.** And He is willing to change His mind about both the hardening and the mercy, if people change. If Gentiles become arrogant and cease walking by faith alone, they will once again be "cut off." And if the Jews who are now hardened will not "persist in their unbelief," God will "graft them in again" (Romans 11:22-23). [Emphasis added]

The ones referred to in Romans 9:23, then – those "whom He prepared in advance for His glory" – is anyone who chooses to believe. Individuals can change their destiny by what they believe. Praise God! And God predetermined that those who choose to believe the Gospel of salvation would be glorified. Romans 9 is not suggesting God predetermined their choices, only that the *results* of their choices is predetermined.

Why a Fatalistic Interpretation of Romans 9 is in Opposition to What Jesus Reveals about the True Nature of God

As with all issues pertaining to proper Bible doctrine, we must base all our theological deliberations on our understanding of the Savior, Jesus Christ. Jesus is the image and perfect expression of the essence of God (Colossians 1:15, Hebrews 1:3) and is even the embodiment of the one and only Word of God (John 1:1). Jesus supersedes all previously-held beliefs about God, and He is the ultimate revelation of the substance of God.

The fatalistic interpretation of Romans 9 is in stark opposition with the God we see revealed in our Savior. Jesus' willingness to complete the plan of salvation by being butchered on a cross for those who sneered at Him reveals the essence of what God is like. God's nature is love and mercy toward all. A fatalistic interpretation of Romans 9, however, forces us to determine this is only partially true of God, because His love applies only to *some* people – those who have been pre-elected. Rather than the magnificent portrayal of the loving God we find demonstrated in Jesus Christ, we instead find a rigid and unmerciful deity who has unilaterally resolved that some would be saved and others would be damned of no fault or merits of their own, all for "his glory." This means the revelation of God we find in Christ is not the final word if the fatalistic interpretation of Romans 9 is true – Jesus doesn't ultimately or definitively reveal the heart of God. Rather, Christ's death on Mt. Calvary actually obscures the nature of God as much as it reveals it.

I'll let the words of Greg Boyd finish out this chapter by again referring to his article "How Do You Respond to Romans 9":

> *If we rather resolve that Jesus is our definitive picture of God, and that this picture cannot be placed alongside of or qualified by any other, then we must conclude that there is something amiss with the deterministic interpretation of Romans 9. For Christ reveals, and the biblical witness confirms, that God's love is universal, His love is impartial, His love is kind, and His love desires all to be saved (e.g. 1 John 4:8; Duet 4:8; Deut 10:17-19; 2 Chron 19:7; Ezek 18:25; Mk 12:14; Jn 3:16; Acts 10:34; Rom 2:10-11; Eph 6:9; 1 Tim 2:4; 1 Peter1:17; 2 Peter 3:9).*
>
> *...I conclude that the deterministic interpretation of Romans 9 is as misguided as it is unfortunate. It is misguided not only because it misinterprets Paul, but because it fundamentally clashes with the supremacy of God's self-revelation in Christ. And it is unfortunate because it tragically replaces the unsurpassably glorious picture of God as Jesus Christ dying on the cross for undeserving sinners with a picture of a deity who defies all moral sensibilities by arbitrarily fashioning certain people to be vessels fit for eternal destruction — and then punishing them for being that way. It exchanges the picture of a beautiful God who reigns supreme with self-sacrificial love and flexible wisdom for a picture of a God who reigns by the arbitrary exercise of sheer power.*
>
> *I unequivocally affirm that the sovereign God "has mercy on whomever He wants to have mercy, and He hardens whomever He wants to harden." I would simply add that the "whomever" He has mercy on refers to "all who choose to believe" while the*

"whomever" He hardens refers to "all who refuse to believe." The passage demonstrates the wisdom of God's loving flexibility, not the sheer determinism of God's power.

9

How God's Kingdom Operates: Is God in Control of Everything?

In light of the previous chapters dealing with predestination, it is noteworthy to reiterate that God's sovereignty refers to Him being supreme in power, wisdom, and authority. It does *not* mean God controls everything. This is probably a shocking statement for some people who have been taught the increasingly popular mantra, "God is in control," which often implies that no matter what happens God is behind it. Therefore, let's examine what God's Word has to say on the subject. If you will keep an open mind, I believe you may see some things in this chapter from God's Word that you may have never considered. In doing so, let us strive to lean on the truth of God's Word rather than traditions of men.

In order to understand eternal security, we must also have a grasp of God's sovereignty and what sovereignty truly means. In this chapter it may seem at first that I'm deviating from the subject of eternal security and the sovereignty of God, but hang in there because I'm leading up to an important point which forms the bedrock of the Gospel and should shape our understanding of the true nature of God.

God Honors a Governmental Code of Spiritual Law

If we are to comprehend what God's sovereignty actually means and how this understanding will shape our view of eternal security and indeed our individual roles in God's Kingdom, we must first realize that God created mankind to rule and reign on the earth.

It was God's objective to give the first people the privilege and responsibility of being His co-rulers. God delegated to Adam and Eve the responsibility of managing and overseeing the Garden, and they were in charge of it (see Genesis 2:15). God conferred upon the man and woman the assignment of administration and cultivation of the world and very likely had in mind for the glory of the Garden to eventually expand and encompass the entire planet as the population multiplied. Some of that delegated authority played out even before Eve was created when God assigned Adam the task of naming all the animals. Whatever Adam named them, that's what they were called because God had delegated authority on the earth to him.

Adam and Eve were acting on God's behalf similar to how the CEO of a Fortune 500 company might delegate authority to his son, allowing him to run the company however he sees fit. Or you might think of it as an arrangement between a renter and a landlord. The landlord owns the property, but the renter has certain rights and responsibilities delegated by the owner. The renter can manage, decorate, and furnish the property however he wants, and the landlord gives him this right.

God is the owner of the planet, but He has given certain rights and privileges to the "renters," which is you and me. And God would likewise honor the choices of the first renters, Adam and Eve.

Tragically, Adam and Eve relinquished their authority to a spiritual outlaw. By rebelling against God and allowing themselves to be seduced by Lucifer, now known as the devil or Satan, Adam and Eve experienced what God had previously promised. He told them if they ever ate of the forbidden tree they would die. Their physical death wasn't immediate, of course, but death was immediately unleashed on the earth in all its vile forms. Similar to how Jacob connived the blessing of the first born away from his brother Esau, Satan connived to steal authority over the earth away from Adam and Eve and became its ruler.

This is why when Satan came to tempt Jesus in the wilderness, he declared the kingdoms of the world had been "delivered" to him and he could in turn give them to anyone he chose (see Luke 4:5-6). The word "delivered" in this text is taken from the Greek word *paradidimoi*, and it describes the act of handing something over to someone else. By disobeying God, Adam effectively delivered or transferred over to Satan the authority of this earth that God had originally assigned to Adam.

Let's again consider our analogy of a renter and landlord. If the owner of an office building leased space to a local business, and the owner of the business allowed a vagrant off the street to come in and stay all day and disrupt business with the customers and eventually start making demands, it would *not* be the landlord's responsibility to throw him out. Rather, it is the responsibility of the person who owns the small business and who is leasing the space. Once the lease is signed, the lessee has jurisdiction of what happens in the space to a large degree from that point forward. If he approached the landlord and said, "Sir, I have a vagrant who has come in off the street and won't leave," the landlord would probably respond, "Well, that's too bad, but it's not my problem; throw him out!" But if the lessee won't throw out the vagrant, and the vagrant continues to feel emboldened and then brings in some big, heavily-armed thugs to help him take over the day-to-day business dealings, then the lessee has abdicated his authority to an unauthorized person. The landlord is not responsibility for the actions or *lack* of actions of the lessee.

Similarly, God signed over the title of planet earth to Adam and Eve, and they, in turn, allowed Satan, a vagrant if you will, to come in and take over. This was not God's perfect will, but He honored that choice. Thus, it was true from that moment forward that "the whole world is under the control of the evil one" (1 John 5:19).

Before the time of Christ, the world was in desperate straits, for a spiritual desperado named Satan had taken control, and he is bent on pure evil. As Jesus said in John 10:10, "the thief comes only to steal and kill and destroy."

The Father saw this world in the clutches of a cruel tyrant who was crushing the life out of His beloved – the same ones in whom He had demonstrated such confidence when He created us and delegated His authority to us. He gave us the commission to rule over this planet as His vice regents, but we lost control of the world to a twisted, perverted, and shrewd fallen angelic being who was now ruling in our place. In response, God immediately put into motion a plan to strip Satan of his rulership – a plan to take the very form of the humans He created and then shedding His own blood in order to free those who trust in Him from the grip of the evil one.

Thus, the reason the Father sent His Son is clearly articulated in First John 3:8:

The reason the Son of God appeared was to destroy the devil's work.

Before the death and resurrection of Jesus, mankind was hopelessly dominated by the devil. His control on the earth was unchallenged. Even Jesus did not contest the fact that Satan had authority over the kingdoms of the earth when Satan tempted Him in the wilderness. Satan said to Jesus regarding the kingdoms of the world, "*I will give you all their authority and splendor; it has been given to me, and I can give it to anyone I want to*" (Luke 4:6). Yet in spite of those rights of ownership which Satan possessed,

Jesus also told His disciples He was now giving them authority to trample on the works of Satan and to overcome all the power of the evil one.

> *Behold, I give you authority to tread on serpents*
> *and scorpions, and over all the power of the enemy.*
> *Nothing will in any way hurt you.*
> -Luke 10:19 (Word English Bible)

When Jesus died on the cross and then descended briefly into hell, a powerful thing happened. The Scriptures tell us that Jesus stripped Satan of the keys to death and hell (see Revelation 1:18). When Jesus returned to briefly to give His disciples further instruction, He told them in Matthew 28:18, just before His ascension back to heaven, that all authority in heaven and earth has now been given to Him, and He was commissioning them to go and enforce His victory by spreading the gospel and advancing God's Kingdom on the earth. He was delegating His power and authority to mankind *yet again* in order to beat back the forces of hell unleashed on the earth.

Jesus explained in more detail how the advancement of His Kingdom is to be accomplished in a short address now known as the Great Commission:

> ¹⁵ **And He said to them, "Go into all the world and preach the gospel to every creature. ¹⁶ He who believes and is baptized will be saved; but he who does not believe will be condemned. ¹⁷ And these signs will follow those who believe: In My name they will cast out demons; they will speak with new tongues; ¹⁸ they will take up serpents; and if they drink anything deadly, it will by no means hurt them; they will lay hands on the sick, and they will recover."**
> -Mark 16:15-18 (NKJV)

As the Creator, God owned the earth and could delegate authority in it to anyone He chose. He bestowed this authority upon the objects of His love, Adam and Eve, instructing them to be fruitful and multiply. As the ones wielding that delegated authority, Adam and Eve then turned it over to Satan, who was in control of the earth until the time of Jesus. And Jesus, in a colossal victory, stripped Satan of that authority and won it back.

But things did not automatically return to the conditions of the Garden.

Demonic forces had already been unleashed on the earth, but now mankind had been empowered with the ability through Jesus Christ and the Holy Spirit to defeat them and cast them down. Although Jesus won back the authority, in a move reminiscent of the Garden, God once again delegated His authority back to mankind and expects us to enforce His victory and appropriate it on the earth. If we learn how to do that, then God's Kingdom advances. If we do not, then **Satan's works go uncontested by those who believe God will do whatever He wants whenever He wants with or without our involvement**.

Although God still owns the earth (see Psalm 24:1), and while authority has been stripped away from Satan and once again delegated back to mankind, Satan has nevertheless become a usurper, or a squatter. A squatter is someone who unlawfully occupies an uninhabited building or unused land, which is a very good description of Satan's usurping of unoccupied territory, or in other words, an earth where mankind has failed to take his rightful place as God's vice-regents.

Hebrews 2:7-8 tells us that God crowned mankind with glory and honor and placed all things under our feet. In the present time we do not see the fulfilment of this reality, however, simply because many people have a faulty understanding of the sovereignty of God and also because the modern Church has been taught to have a heaven mentality instead of a Kingdom mentality. In other words, we are just looking to the sky waiting for Jesus to come and take us all away instead of being busy advancing His Kingdom until the day Jesus comes back. We are a generation with an escapist mindset rather than an "occupy" mindset. We are like the servant with the one mina in Luke 19.

In Jesus' parable in Luke 19, we are told of a servant who instead of putting the master's money to work while the master was away like he had been commissioned, hid the money in the ground, which cost him dearly when the master returned. Jesus' express purpose for teaching this parable was to warn us that we had better be about the Father's business while we have time. He said, "occupy until I come" (v. 13). The word *occupy* as it is translated in the King James, is the Greek word *pragmateuomai* which is where we get the word *pragmatic*, and it means *to busy one's self*. The implication is that God does not want us to have a lazy, escapist mentality like the servant with the one mina. He wants us to busy ourselves with appropriating His victory at Calvary and advancing His Kingdom on the earth.

The Church has been given power to throw the devil out of the earth realm forever and replace his dark kingdom with the Kingdom of Light. Instead, we have been trying to get out of here ourselves. As my friend and mentor, Dr. Jerry King, has said, "God has been trying to get on the planet and the Church has been trying get off it."

Jesus didn't preach Heaven nearly as much as He preached the Kingdom, which may come as a surprise to many readers. Yet the Kingdom is mentioned 128 times in the gospels alone. The advancement of His Kingdom was Jesus' primary message, but most Christians believe His primary concern was just getting people to Heaven. Getting people to Heaven was of primary importance to be sure, but Jesus' bigger concern was getting His disciples to appropriate the authority we have been given so the works of Satan would be crushed. Over and over Jesus tried to get His disciples to do what they had seen Him do and even rebuked them for their unbelief when they failed. When Jesus delegated His authority just before His ascension, the early Church took this seriously. In fact, the first four centuries of the Church advanced the Kingdom with such power that miracles were commonplace, and they literally overtook the Roman Empire in the 4th Century.

Why, then, has the modern Church become so weak by comparison? It's because we are so heavenly minded that we have become no earthly good, to quote a popular saying. **We have become too preoccupied with selfish pursuits just waiting around to get to heaven and have lost the priority of advancing God's Kingdom in the here and now as our primary concern. And one reason for this faulty mentality is the belief that God's will is already being accomplished with or without our involvement.**

Starting from the time of the Fall until this present day, God is honoring the choices of His people to whom He has delegated His authority in order to decimate the forces of hell that have been occupying this planet for the last 6,000 years. Therefore, contrary to what some people believe and teach, God is not ordaining everything happening on earth. The trouble, pain, and turmoil we see in the world is the work of Satan, not God. If anyone needs proof of a real demonic realm, just look around at the work of Satan's kingdom. The world is full of it, and it vexes God when His people do not use the authority delegated to us to overcome Satan's evil work. God has entrusted the Church with the task of kicking Satan out.

Although hell's dominion has been thoroughly vanquished by Jesus' finished work on the cross, Satan and his legions of demons are nevertheless carrying out tactical guerilla warfare. This is why Satan is referred to in Second Corinthians 4:4 as the "god of this world." He controls the systems of this world and is still carrying out his demonic plans when God's people do not rise up and resist him. But when we do, James 4:7 says he will flee.

God Has Voluntarily Limited Himself to Work within the Context of Partnership

To reiterate, God's sovereignty does not mean He controls every detail of everything happening on earth. The dictionary definition of sovereignty simply states, "supreme in power and authority." A sovereign nation, for example, simply means that its government is autonomous and supreme in authority within its borders. But that sovereignty doesn't mean the government is controlling every action, every decision, and every circumstance of its citizens. This understanding of sovereignty is consistent with the Biblical definition of how God operates. He is supreme in power, wisdom, and authority, but He is not controlling every detail, decision, action and circumstance of the world. He didn't do that in the Garden when life was perfect, and He isn't doing it now. God honors free will.

Therefore, taking back territory from Satan is not something God is simply going to come swooping in to do without the involvement of His vice-regents, which are you and me. God could do so if He chose, but if He did, He would violate the arrangement He made with mankind. We are still His co-laborers, and He will work only within the context of the prayers, decrees, and labor of His people.

For this reason, the Bible says the ancient Israelites "limited the Holy One of Israel" (Psalm 78:41, KJV). Other translations say they "vexed" God. **If God is the One arranging all the details behind the scenes in the first place, how then can He be displeased by the bad choices people make?** God wanted the Israelites to make a short trip from Egypt to enter the Promised Land, but their stubborn refusal to go in and take the land away from the wicked Canaanites thwarted that desire and plan, and it limited God's ability to complete His plan in the desired time frame because He was working within the context of the faith and cooperation of the Israelites. Thus, He was "limited" in His ability to help them, which vexed Him.

In contrast to this truth, some people will say, "Well, I believe since God is all-powerful, He will do whatever He pleases regardless of what mankind does."

No, that's not how His Kingdom works. He didn't set it up that way. God *is* all-powerful indeed, but remember, even though the Bible tells us God does not wish for anyone to perish but that everyone would come to repentance, this is not what happens. *Everyone* doesn't repent. Masses of people rebel against Him and go to their destruction. Yet He desires them to turn and repent.

God is indeed all-knowing and all-powerful, but in His sovereignty, He has limited Himself to the choices, prayers, petitions, faith, and actions of the people on earth. If everything was predetermined without the involvement of God's people, what benefit would there be in prayer and evangelism? None. God works through the delegated authority of His people. Yes, He does direct the courses of our lives to an extent; we are not autonomous beings. But God will not override mankind's free will and force us to do things we would never have otherwise done. We have to cooperate with God, and when we do, He intervenes in marvelous ways.

The Apostle Peter spoke to this:

> *¹⁴This is the confidence we have in approaching God: that if we ask anything according to his will, He hears us. ¹⁵And if we know that He hears us— whatever we ask—we know that we have what we asked of Him.*
> *-1 Peter 5:14-15*

What's the point of this verse? There has to be knowledge of God's will through His written Word, and there needs to be corresponding action, which in this case is the asking. The implication here is that without the asking there will be no divine response. The very fact Jesus taught His disciples to pray for God's Kingdom to come and His will would be done on earth as it is in heaven assumes God's perfect will is not accomplished without the earnest prayers of His people. Thus, God acts only when His people pray. (See Matthew 6:9-10, 2 Chronicles 7:14.) He partners with you and me.

James follows suit:

> *⁶When you ask, you must believe and not doubt, because the one who doubts is like a wave of the sea, blown and tossed by the wind. ⁷That person should not expect to receive anything from the Lord. ⁸Such a person is double-minded and unstable in all they do.*
>
> *-James 1:6-8*

"Wait. You're saying God won't answer prayers if I don't ask in faith?"

No, I didn't say that. The Bible said it. James 1:6-8 and 1 Peter 5:14-15 taken together tell us we must pray in order to see God act. But prayer must be combined with faith and knowledge of His will. Without those three ingredients – prayer, knowledge, and faith – then Scripture tells us we should not expect to get anything. Again, I didn't say that; God did.

God is not "sovereign" in the sense He is just going to do whatever He wants to do whenever He wants to do it. He could if He chose, but that's not how the Word says He operates. We have to partner with Him, and when we do, this is when we see results. We can't just do whatever we want and expect we are still in the perfect will of God. The Father ordained the writing of His Word so we could know His will and live in it (see Ephesians 1:9). On the other hand, if a person doesn't know God's will and doesn't live according to it then God's perfect will is not accomplished.

God wants to partner with His people in order to advance His Kingdom and His will throughout the earth. People who believe God is just going to do whatever He wants and we have no involvement or responsibility in the matter, however, have taken the default position of being blown here and there by whatever circumstance happens to come along, and they have been deceived into believing they must be pleased with whatever calamity or wickedness raises its ugly head, because, after all, it must be God's will, right?

To illustrate my point, consider the millions of innocent babies who have died at the hands of abortion doctors. This surely grieves the heart of God, who said, "Before I formed you in the womb, I knew you" (Jeremiah 1:5). God did not ordain abortion; it is a work of Satan. Fortunately, the tide has begun to turn against the abortion industry. Planned Parenthood has been under heavy fire and scrutiny at the time of this writing, and the number of abortions performed each year has declined sharply since 1990. Society is becoming more aware of the horror of abortion and the sanctity of preborn life. Why? It's because of the sustained prayers and mammoth efforts of God's people who have felt the pain of the Father's heart and undertaken His work. In fact, Planned Parenthood's own statistics show that the no-show rate for scheduled abortion patients goes up to 75% when there are people praying near the clinics when women arrive for their procedures. Isn't that amazing? God works through the prayers and efforts of His people! He is not a Lone Ranger. He wants to partner with you and me!

The Worst Heresy Ever?

The way some circles are teaching about the sovereignty of God grants people a certain amount of comfort about troubling situations in life that are difficult to explain or understand, like my business client I mentioned in the introduction. However, there are many false teachings that provide the same sense of comfort and false security. Satan must sprinkle in a certain amount of truth with every lie in order to avoid detection, and false doctrine must also possess the offer of peace and security in order to gain wide appeal. This is the nature of false doctrine. If it were easy to detect, no one would believe it. And if it were not attractive, no one would embrace it.

The fact is, the sovereignty of God the way it has been taught in many religious circles has been referred to by some as the worst heresy in the history of the Church for two reasons:

First, it misrepresents the nature of God since it implies He is the author of all manner of human suffering. Isn't that shrewd of Satan? He inflicts untold suffering on the subjects of God's love and then figures out a way to blame it on God and get people to believe it. Satan truly is a liar and an accuser! He not only whispers accusations in the ears of God's people in order to keep us trapped in cycles of shame, but he also makes accusations against God to you and me. He's been doing that since the time of Adam and Eve, attempting to deceive people about the nature of our Father.

Secondly, the sovereignty of God the way it's currently being taught tends to excuse people from any personal responsibility, which is what the concept of unconditional eternal security does. Pastor Keith Moore of Branson, Missouri calls the popular version of the sovereignty of God "no fault religion." In other words, "whatever happens, it's not my fault, because it must have been God's plan." This has been a very effective satanic strategy in hindering the advancement of God's Kingdom.

Have you ever considered that people who believe this way don't even practice their own convictions? Consider sickness as an example.

Many believe God puts sickness on His people in order to teach them character or patience, even though there is zero scriptural evidence to support this belief. Certainly, God in His rich mercy can teach people things in the midst of sickness, and He can demonstrate different facets of His love and character to people who are suffering, but this is in *response* to the sickness, not because of it. I often like to say that God is an opportunist; He will use whatever is at His disposal to minister to His people. But the idea of God maiming people and striking His beloved with sickness and disease to teach them character cannot be supported in the Bible. Whenever God smote someone with sickness in the Bible, such as when He struck Moses' sister Miriam with leprosy, it was always as an act of judgment; it was never a "blessing in disguise." The same ones who claim God makes people sick to teach them humility or to bless them in some unseen way will immediately go to the doctor to receive care in the hopes of getting better whenever they fall ill. So then, **if they believe it is God's will for them to be sick, yet they respond by doing everything they can to get better, then they either don't really believe it's God will for them to be sick, or else they are knowingly and purposefully attempting to circumvent God's will by trying to get better even though they believe He wants them to be sick, all the while claiming to be suffering for Jesus.**

If people truly believe it is God's will for them to suffer sickness, then the noble and godly thing to do would simply be to accept the suffering and be happy about it and stop trying to get well. The deformed understanding of the sovereignty of God, however, has been a very effective strategy of Satan to get people to accept sickness as hand-delivered by God instead of a result of a sin-soaked world. As a result, people attribute to God what is a work of Satan because they have not learned what the Scriptures say about divine healing and the true nature of God.

God Holds Us Accountable for Our Own Personal Development

"No fault religion" is the way many Christians live their lives due to a distorted understanding of the sovereignty of God and unconditional eternal security. The fact is we *do* have personal responsibility to seek God with all of our hearts (1 Chronicles 16:11), to walk in His ways (Deuteronomy 30:16), and to be busy about His business (Matthew 28:19-20). It is our responsibility to know His Word (2 Timothy 2:15), to pray continually (1 Thessalonians 5:17), and to keep fellowship with God's people in public worship (Hebrews 10:25). It is likewise our responsibility to grow mature in the things of God (2 Peter 1:5-9). God will not do these things for us. He commands *us* to do them, and He blesses us and uses us in response. If we do not do them, however, then our progress is stunted, our effectiveness for the Kingdom is limited, we continue to be dominated by sin and self-destructive mindsets, and we run the risk of falling away from the faith altogether.

Many Christians, especially American Christians, live very passive spiritual lives. Their idea of being a disciple of Jesus Christ is reading their Bible once in a while, praying now and then, going to church when they feel like it, and not committing the "big" sins like adultery. As long as they do that, their consciences are appeased. Yet this is not what true Christianity looks like. Being a disciple of Jesus Christ means "taking up your cross" to follow Christ, to quote Jesus. Consider carefully His sober words:

> *²⁴Then Jesus said to His disciples, "Whoever wants to be my disciple must deny themselves and take up their cross and follow me. ²⁵For whoever wants to save their life will lose it, but whoever loses their life for me will find it."*
> *-Matthew 16:24-25*

Taking up one's cross is a picture of the execution of a self-focused existence. Being a disciple of Jesus Christ means being consumed with pursuing the things of God as a matter of lifestyle. It is a proactive kind of spiritual life, not a passive one. It also means taking personal responsibility for one's actions and spiritual growth and not chalking up everything that happens as God's will regardless of what you did or did not do.

The whole concept of unconditional eternal security and the sovereignty of God in the way it's being taught in some circles is a very convenient way for some people to live any way they want and exonerate themselves of any conviction to pursue God passionately. They believe they are in God's will regardless of what they do and their eternity is safe and secure. It gives people false hope and a false standard of Christian living.

This is one major reason why it's being called one of the worst heresies in Church history.

It reminds me of the Psalm 36:1-2:

> ¹*There is an oracle in my heart concerning the sinfulness of the wicked.* ²*There is no fear of God in his eyes, for in his eyes he flatters himself too much to hate or detect his sin.*

For many people, eternal security and the false version of the sovereignty of God is a great way to anesthetize the conscience so there is no fear of God and no ability to detect one's sin, let alone hate it. By claiming God controls everything and even one's own spiritual apathy must be His will, we have effectively handed any power or authority we may have had right back to Satan.

Friends, God is not *making* you or me do anything outside of our own wills. He is therefore not dictating our decisions. As such, He is also not dictating our eternal destinies. We have to make a conscious choice to follow His plan, do things His way, and persevere in our faith. Only then are we eternally secure.

10

Eternal Security and Grace

Some proponents of unconditional eternal security argue that *conditional salvation* flies in the face of grace. Their mantra is, "Once a child, always a child." Just as a baby cannot become unborn once he is born, a child of God cannot become born-again and then be unborn-again, according to their reasoning. Therefore, according to this philosophy, once a person is saved, he or she will always be saved. Author Hal Lindsey sums up this way of thinking with his statement:

> *When you're born into a family, you may be a winner or a loser in your behavior, but you're still a member of that family. There's no way to be unborn just because you don't measure up to the standards of your family. It's just the same when you're born into God's family. You may be disciplined for wrong behavior, but you won't be disowned.*

One could fairly apply Lindsey's statements to a Christian who is struggling to overcome a certain sin habit and still falls into it once in a great while. He mourns when it happens and immediately seeks forgiveness, but his life is characterized by a strained effort toward holiness. However, Lindsey's remark misses the mark when applied to those who willfully live a life of disobedience, such as would be the case with someone who is sexually immoral, for example, since the Bible clearly states that fornicators (those who engage in pre-marital sex), adulterers, and homosexuals will not inherit the kingdom of God (1 Corinthians 6:9,10). Paul calls those kinds of people "wicked." Only a *perversion* of grace allows for sexual immorality, because true grace *"teaches us to say NO to ungodliness and worldly passions and to live self-controlled, upright, and godly lives in this present age"* (Titus 2:12).

The argument of "once a child, always a child," is based upon a physical, biological argument, not a spiritual one. If we were to limit our understanding of spiritual things to the biological or natural, we would have to assume that since we are born to one father, we could never be separated from him. That father would *always* be our father, and we would have no other even if we wanted one. The Bible describes those who are outside the grace of God as "children of the devil" (Acts 13:10, 1 John 3:10) and "sons of the evil one" (Matthew 13:38). If we were to adhere to the same "once-a-child-always-a-child" reasoning, we would have to assume NO ONE could be saved, because we are all children of Satan and that cannot change. Praise God, it CAN and DOES change for those who place their faith in Christ.

Just as Nicodemus had trouble understanding Jesus' statements about being "born again" because he was trying to comprehend it from a natural, carnal perspective (see John 3:1-10), we must not attempt to understand spiritual things from a purely physical, carnal perspective. When Jesus declared to Nicodemus, *"I tell you the truth, no one can see the kingdom of God unless he is born again,"* Nicodemus was listening with his carnal understanding. He replied, *"How can a man be born when he is old? Surely he cannot enter a second time into his mother's womb to be born!"* Nicodemus did not understand what Jesus was talking about because he was limiting his thinking to the physical, and Jesus was speaking of the spiritual.

Some advocates of the eternal security doctrine use this same natural reasoning when they ask the rhetorical question, *"Can you be born again, again?"*

This terminology has confused people because being "born again" is the same as "getting saved" or believing in Jesus. In short, it simply means to receive and experience salvation. If one could stop believing in Jesus then later start believing again, he would indeed get saved again, as Romans 11:22-23 declares:

> ²²***Behold then the kindness and severity of God; to those who fell, severity, but to you, God's kindness, IF YOU CONTINUE in His kindness; OTHERWISE YOU ALSO SHALL BE CUT OFF.*** ²³***And they also, IF THEY DO NOT CONTINUE IN THEIR UNBELIEF, WILL BE GRAFTED IN AGAIN, FOR GOD IS ABLE TO GRAFT THEM IN AGAIN.***

So yes, according to Scripture, a person can receive salvation, stop believing and be "cut off," then come to his senses and believe again and be "grafted in again." This, in fact, is exactly what happened with the prodigal son. The Scriptures say in Luke 15:24-32 that he became "alive again."

In fact, I am one of those people who was grafted in again. I made my first public profession of faith at age 14, and I lived a fairly clean Christian life until the age of 21. It was then my lack of spiritual discipline caught up to me, and I plunged headlong into a hard-living 6-year prodigal experience that eventually led me to verbally and publicly renouncing Christ. But, thank God, I came to my senses in the spring of 1992 and repented of my sin in tears, and God took me back in. His grace knows no end!

The question, "Can a Christian be born again, again?" is a rhetorical question. It is asked simply for effect. It does not work to bolster an otherwise weak argument that has no basis in God's Word.

So, too, we must ask the Holy Spirit of God to enlighten our understanding so we can see with spiritual eyes and hear with spiritual ears and understand with a spiritual mind. Otherwise, things we see in the Bible that appear difficult or contradictory will *never* make sense to us, and we will not benefit from them. If we rely solely on natural analogies to explain and understand the spiritual, very little revelation will come to us regarding some of the more complex matters pertaining to the supernatural. We can never hope to understand the Trinity this side of heaven, for example, and one can ever use natural examples, as I have heard some attempt to do, to explain this great mystery. Likewise, the natural cannot explain the law of reciprocity (give and you shall receive), the infinite existence of God, or the miracles of Jesus. Unless the Christian has a firm conviction that natural law is superseded by higher, supernatural laws, then it is very difficult, if not impossible, to live by faith, for *"faith is being sure of what we hope for, and confident of what we do not see"* (Hebrews 11:6).

I reiterate, therefore, that **eternal security is not a true grace teaching, because the grace of God will result in a progressively more godly life.** Consider well the words of Holy Scripture on that point:

> **[11]The grace of God has appeared that offers salvation to all people. [12]It teaches us to say "No" to ungodliness and worldly passions, and live a self-controlled, upright and godly life in this present age.**
> **-Titus 2:11-12**

Did you catch that? Grace isn't just about getting the mercy you don't deserve. **Grace, if genuinely embraced, has a purifying effect**. In other words, a person cannot genuinely experience the grace of God and simply go on living in sin. A person who has truly experienced salvation through faith in Jesus Christ will have a desire to please the Savior, because grace has begun doing its job of instructing in righteousness.

On that note, let's look again at a foundational verse to our faith, and then read it in context.

> [8]*For it is by grace you have been saved, through faith – and this is not from yourselves, it is a gift of God –* [9]*not by works, so that no one can boast.*
> *-Ephesians 2:8-9*

This is a wonderful truth, and many Christians can quote this passage from memory. The very next verse, however, is intended to be read as a continuation of this thought.

> *For we are God's workmanship, created in Christ Jesus to do good works, which God prepared in advance for us to do.* (v. 10)

If we read all three verses as they were intended to be read, as a connected thought, then **we must conclude that grace truly embraced will result in good works**. And if good works and a change in one's lifestyle are not evident, then by implication this passage is also bolstering truths taught elsewhere in the Bible: **salvation has not been experienced if there is no resulting fruit to show its genuineness**.

Yes, grace not only gives us the mercy we don't deserve and withholds the judgment we do deserve, but equally true is that grace is empowering; it gives us the desire to live godly and empowers us to change. Advocates of an unconditional eternal security doctrine deny this truth, however, because they teach that a person can experience the grace of God and then later begin living in all manner of sin and perversion and still be saved.

Pay close attention to the words of author, Bible teacher, and vocal opponent of the eternal security doctrine, Jeff Paton:

> *The eternal security doctrine is rooted in unbelief, seeing that they deny that Christ has any power to deliver the believer here and now. The Bible tells us that Jesus came to destroy the works of the devil, and that Jesus came to save His people FROM their sin, not IN their sins. A savior who cannot live up to his promise to deliver us from our sins in this life cannot be depended upon to deliver us after our death.*

If we have truly experienced the salvation of God and are holding fast to our profession of faith, and if we truly love Christ, we will be compelled to love what He loves and hate what He hates. We will desire more than anything else to please Him and to follow in His footsteps. On the occasions we do stumble it will grieve us, and we will seek immediate repentance. We will constantly be growing in maturity and discovering new areas of weakness and sin for which we purpose in our hearts to repent of and submit to God's Word. Our lives will constantly be going through a metamorphosis of change year by year. We will love the house of God, love His Word, be devoted to prayer, and will earnestly desire others to be saved and escape judgment. If these things are not apparent in a person's life, serious evaluation of one's spiritual condition to determine if he or she is in the faith is in order, because there is a good chance he or she is not. God's grace is not an excuse for an apathetic spiritual life. In fact, Jesus in Revelation 3:15-16 says the following of spiritual apathy:

> **[15]I know your deeds, that you are neither cold nor hot. I wish you were one or the other! [16]So, because you are lukewarm – neither hot nor cold – I am about to spit you out of my mouth.**

This verse is impossible to reconcile with an eternal security doctrine, since it was addressed to a *church*, not unbelievers.

Jesus was essentially saying, *your spiritual apathy makes me sick, and I'm about to vomit you out.* God's grace does not appear to cover spiritual apathy among believers, according to this verse. That's why Jesus also said the road of salvation is a "narrow" one, and few – yes, few – would find it (Matthew 7:13-14). He also said many "good" religious people will come to Him on the Day of Judgment expecting to receive His grace and salvation but will instead receive damnation (Matthew 7:21-23).

Grace simply means "unmerited favor." None of us deserve salvation, and we did nothing based upon human endeavor to earn it. However, we obviously *did* have to do *something* to receive it, which was to acknowledge we are sinners and have violated God's commands and are deserving of His judgment; we had to repent of our sins; we had to place our faith and trust in Jesus. Just as these acts of belief allowed us to take advantage of the wonderful gift of salvation, subsequent acts of *unbelief* – those who reject what was previously held sacred – can forfeit that salvation. In fact, it has been suggested by some Bible scholars that the truest definition of taking the Lord's Name in vain does not necessarily have to do with profanity. The ultimate taking of the Lord's Name in vain is identifying yourself with God by your words or by a religious ceremony but then living as if you have no regard for Him.

The wonderful message of the gospel is that because we have all sinned and fallen short of God's standards, none of us can get to heaven based upon our own righteousness. Jesus therefore bridged the gap based upon His righteousness on behalf of those who place their faith (*pisteuo* – John 3:16) in Him and who cling to Him through obedience (John 14:15). As long as we are repentant and faithful, grace covers us. Conversely, if we become unfaithful, and if we fall back into a life of unrepentant carnality, the Scriptures are clear that we have trampled God's grace and have removed ourselves from the covering of His mercy, thus placing ourselves back under a curse, as the following passages unmistakably point out:

²⁶*Dear friends, if we continually keep on sinning after we have received a full knowledge of the truth, there is no other sacrifice that will cover these sins.* ²⁷*There will be nothing to look forward to but the terrible expectation of God's judgment and the raging fire that will consume His enemies.* ²⁸*Anyone who refused to obey the Law of Moses was put to death without mercy on the testimony of two or three witnesses.* ²⁹*Think how much more terrible the punishment will be for those who have trampled on the son of God and have treated the blood of the covenant as if it were common and unholy. Such people have insulted and enraged the Holy Spirit who brings God's mercy to His people.* ³⁰*For we know the One who said, "I will take vengeance. I will repay those who deserve it." He also said, "The Lord will judge His own people."* ³¹*It is a terrible thing to fall into the hands of the living God...*

-Hebrews 10:26-31

²⁰*If they have escaped the corruption of the world by knowing our Lord and Savior Jesus Christ and are again entangled in it and overcome, they are worse off at the end that they were at the beginning.* ²¹*It would have been better for them to not to have known the way of righteousness, than to have known it and then to turn their backs on the sacred command that was passed on to them.* ²²*Of them the proverbs are true: "A dog returns to its vomit," and, "A sow that is washed goes back to her wallowing in the mud."*

-2 Peter 2:20-22

Clearly, the Word of God gives absolutely no indication that a person can receive Christ as Savior and then later begin living in unrestrained immorality and still be covered by His grace, as some eternal security advocates seem to believe. Some even consider those who renounce Christ and embrace atheism are still saved if they once received Christ as Lord. This is a heresy!

As discussed earlier, others claim that a person who turns away after once repenting was never saved to begin with. I must ask, though, *where's God's grace in that?* If someone knelt at an altar and poured his heart out to God in repentance, would God refuse to hear and respond? Of course not! The Scriptures say God does not want anyone to perish but wishes all to come to repentance (2 Peter 3:9). Romans 10:9 proclaims God's grace when Paul wrote that *anyone* who confesses Jesus as Lord and believes in his heart that God raised Him from the dead would be saved, and Acts 2:21 assures us that *all* who call on the Lord shall be saved. The Bible doesn't say *some* people who call on the Lord and believe Jesus was raised from the dead shall be saved. It says *all of them would be saved.* God is not in the business of turning away any who call on Him and suggesting He does is a perversion of the gospel.

Many eternal security advocates understandably wish to exalt God's grace. In doing so, however, they inadvertently pervert it by suggesting God will not hear the prayers of some repentant people but will allow all manner of perversity and evil in others to go un-judged. For this reason, I must say respectfully but without apology to eternal security devotees that their doctrine is not one of grace; it is a mutation of the gospel bearing no resemblance to what the Bible teaches.

If I had to choose to err on the side of one extreme or the other, it would be better to run the risk of teaching a doctrine that makes some believers feel insecure in their salvation than to teach a doctrine that gives non-believers false confidence. In this present age, it is the tendency of modern Christendom to create cheap grace, wanting to give assurance to those who do not love Jesus.

This tendency isn't new; it is just more widely accepted today. Centuries ago, Martin Luther wrote the following:

> *Satan, the god of all dissension, stirs up daily new sects, the latest of which I would have never foreseen or once suspected. He has raised up a sect such that teaches that men should not be terrified by the Law, but gently exalted by the teaching of the grace of Christ.*

Charles Finney likewise observed this:

> *Evermore the Law must prepare the way for the gospel. To overlook this in instructing souls is almost certain to result in false hope, the introduction of a false standard of Christian experience, and to fill the church with false converts.*

If we have no regard for God's Law and do not tremble when we compare ourselves to it, then we cannot experience His grace. The Law cannot save us, but it is there to show us how far short we fall of God's standards so we may gain an appreciation for His grace and trust Jesus as our Savior (Romans 3:19-22).

God's grace is wonderful, and God's hand of mercy is not too short to reach even the most heinous of sinners. However, His grace is clearly conditional. As long as we remain faithful, nothing we have done in our past can keep us from enjoying the amazing gift of salvation. If we do not remain faithful, though, we have *removed ourselves* from this blessed hope.

11

Is the Eternal Security Doctrine an Apostate Teaching?

Some claim that the eternal security doctrine is an apostate teaching resulting in the loss of one's soul just for believing or teaching it. I would take exception.

Here's what we know for sure about salvation and what both camps agree upon:

1. We have all violated God's commandments and are therefore under the penalty of His wrath apart from grace.
2. We, therefore, cannot earn our salvation by our deeds because all of us have already broken God's Laws and must pay the penalty.
3. Jesus came to earth as a representation of God Himself in the form of lowly man in order to take upon Himself His own punishment for sin. He became the substitutionary sacrifice so those who trust Him for salvation can go free.
4. Salvation, therefore, is a free gift of grace.
5. Salvation is received by faith and not a result of one's own merits.

Let's say, for example, that someone becomes a Christian and is living by faith. Perhaps this convert is in love with Jesus, has repented of his sinful lifestyle, is in fellowship with other believers, and is living a life of submission to the commandments of God. What if this same person believes a once-saved-always-saved doctrine? Does this cancel out his faith? I do not see evidence of that in the Scriptures. Let's ask, though, if the false doctrine in which he believes has the ability to stunt his spiritual growth and weaken his faith? Yes, the *potential* is there, and thus, the eternal security doctrine, as it appears to me, is heresy, but not apostate.

Heresy is any false teaching having the potential to negatively affect the growth and development of the believer, whereas apostasy is any belief resulting in damnation. Webster's Dictionary defines both as follows:

> **Heresy:** *1) adherence to a religious opinion contrary to church dogma, 2) an opinion, doctrine, or practice contrary to the truth or to generally accepted beliefs or standards.*
> **Apostasy:** *1) renunciation of a religious faith, 2) abandonment of a previous loyalty: defection.*

One can commit some heresies and still be a Christian.

One example of a heresy is the idea that churches should refrain from using instruments of any kind in their worship services since instruments are not mentioned in the New Testament. This concept is clearly in violation of the Scriptures as a whole since the Old Testament is full of references to instruments and the New Testament has no prohibition against them. This curious belief has the potential to diminish the enjoyment from one's worship life and thus interfere with the adoration toward the Father to which music can contribute. God gave us music for a reason, and to deny its importance in the act of corporate or even private worship is to potentially prevent a believer from enjoying some of the blessings of God. As hindering as this belief can be, however, it will not compromise anyone's salvation. Therefore, it is not apostate.

Apostasy, on the other hand, is a deviation from and perversion of the gospel message, which always results in damnation.

An example of apostasy is the teaching that Jesus was simply a good religious teacher who represented one of the many ways to God. This teaching denies the divinity of our Lord Jesus and ignores God's Word which declares Jesus as the only way to the Father. Therefore, those who embrace this deception are not part of His Kingdom.

We examined another apostate teaching already at the outset of our discussion when we studied the book of Galatians. Some of the Christians in Galatia were falling prey to a teaching which suggested salvation could only be experienced by belief in Jesus *as well as observe Jewish laws and customs.* This teaching is apostate because it denies the sufficiency of Jesus' sacrifice on the cross on its own to save mankind, and when one relies on any religious observation to be saved, faith has not been fully placed in Christ, and therefore, salvation has not been experienced.

I know many people who ardently believe in the once-saved-always-saved doctrine but who are passionately and consistently pursuing their relationship with Christ. I am persuaded these people are saved. However, I believe their faulty doctrine is potentially dangerous to them and the people to whom they teach it because it potentially removes the fear of God, which the Bible says is the beginning of all wisdom (Proverbs 1:7) and will keep a person from sin (Proverbs 16:6). A lack of the fear of God makes one vulnerable to sin when tempted. Many who lack any contrition over their sins in the first place will latch on to the eternal security teaching with enthusiasm because it gives them a license to continue in their wicked, self-indulged lifestyles. They think as long as they say a "sinner's prayer," get baptized, appease their consciences by going to church fairly regularly, and say an ingenuous "sorry" to God when they sin, they will go to heaven. For those who truly came to God with repentant hearts but who later left the church and their devotion to Christ because they got discouraged, disgruntled, or swayed back into a life of immorality, there is often no fear of eternal consequences because they were given a promise of eternal security.

Therefore, while those who are *devoted to Christ* but who teach an eternal security doctrine are themselves presently in the faith, they still have blood on their hands. This blood is the blood of the precious ones who fell away and have no conviction to return to their "first love" because of what they have been taught by eternal security teachers. It is also the blood of those who never came to a saving faith in the first place because they thought all they had to do was go through a ritual and they were eternally secure. Those who teach these things which result in the damnation of souls for whom Christ died must one day answer for their heresies.

While I know plenty of eternal security advocates who love Jesus and who are clinging to His commands, I also know even more who use the doctrine to excuse their own spiritual apathy and luke-warmness and who use it to justify their beloved sins which they do not want to give up. To reiterate how Jesus feels about apathy take a look again at what He had to say to the Laodicean church in the third chapter of Revelation:

> [15]*I know your deeds, that you are neither hot nor cold. I wish you were one or the other! So, because you are lukewarm – neither hot nor cold – I am about to spit you out of my mouth. [16]You say, "I am rich; I have acquired wealth and do not need a thing. But you do not realize that you are wretched, pitiful, poor, blind, and naked.* (vv. 15, 16)

Consider this: If I asked myself how much I could sin against my wife without her divorcing me, wouldn't you rightly question my love for her? If in my heart I wanted to be immoral with other women and ignore her needs and only use her for my pleasure and convenience, you would justifiably accuse me of having a very twisted concept of love. It is the same with those who use the doctrine of eternal security to feel secure in thumbing their noses at God's commands and not feel any prick of conviction in doing so. According to Scripture, these kinds of people do not really love Christ, because love for Christ means keeping His commands (John 14:15).

It is because of my concern for these dear ones who teach this doctrine and for those who believe it that I have gone to the trouble to address this issue. Allow me to implore anyone reading this who may be an advocate of unconditional eternal security to pray for insight and wisdom in understanding what the Lord is saying to us in His Word about this all-important issue. If you are wrong, wouldn't you want to know about it *now* rather than in eternity?

Allow me to appeal to you from the standpoint of logic. If you live out the doctrine of eternal security and then find yourself after death standing before the Judgment Seat of God only to find out you were wrong, you may then experience significant loss of reward according to the book of Revelation, if you are even saved at all, depending on how you lived your life. If, though, you live your life believing eternal security is false and you aspire to live a holy life but find out in heaven that you were wrong, you are still safe because you were unconditionally secure and did not know it.

In his article, *Eternal Security and Logic*, Jeff Paton writes:

> The irony of it all is that the content of the letters I receive from those who disagree with me on this matter, is that they chime out with accusations of salvation by "works" and charges of "legalism." Bitter rebukes and suggestions that I am 'lost' are strewn throughout these letters. The irony of this is that these are from those who believe in eternal security! They act as if you can commit adultery, abuse drugs,

rape and murder, and still be a child of God! But yet, if you contend for holiness and living a godly life, you are lost and not eternally secure! According to the Bible, the sin of legalism is just as damning as license! But from the logic of eternal security, it is faith in their doctrine, and not Christ, that saves you! This is proven by the fact that **they do not believe their own doctrine by claiming that a legalist is lost!** *I used to believe in eternal security but I don't anymore; doesn't this mean that I would still be secure, even if I became an ardent legalist according to the logic of this doctrine?* **It is of the utmost hypocrisy to say that we can commit the most heinous crimes and be safe and secure, and at the same time, treat as enemies of the cross those that love God and feel obligated to obey Him! If eternal security were true, then the attitude towards legalism and license should not matter, for they are both sins.** *(emphasis added)*

12

Don't Take My Word on It

I appeal to all who read this: do not take my word as final. I believe I have set forth in this discussion a fair, balanced, and thorough review of Scripture, and I believe I have shown in no uncertain terms what God's Word has to say about eternal security. However, I encourage you to open your Bible yourself and also take advantage of other helpful study tools such as the *Strong's Exhaustive Concordance* and a Bible Commentary of some sort. Likewise, there are numerous materials addressing this issue from both the perspective of the eternal security doctrine and those who oppose it. You can find many of these materials online simply by doing an internet search under "eternal security" or "once saved always saved."

Should you embark upon your own study of both sides of this doctrine, I believe what you will find are "studies" in support of eternal security that simply skim the surface of the verses in question and do not really attempt to do as we have done here and study them in depth. The studies supporting a *conditional* salvation, however, are usually extremely detailed. Case in point: Daniel D. Corner's book *The Believer's Conditional Security* is by far the most comprehensive study of this subject, boasting an incredible 801 pages. His book is available online at Amazon or other similar outlets, or by calling 1-877-428-3746.

Another helpful book is *Programmed by God or Free to Choose* by Dudley Ward, which addresses Calvinism in depth, particularly as it pertains to the sovereignty of God. Ward's book also delivers a great amount of detail about the life and character of John Calvin.

God at War, by Gregory A. Boyd, is another good choice to help better understand the sovereignty of God in relation to evil in the world. Boyd's provocative book deconstructs Calvinism indirectly simply by demonstrating how God's Kingdom operates in contrast to Satan's realm.

The Scriptures say to "*study to show thyself approved unto God, a workman that needeth not to be ashamed, rightly dividing the word of truth*" (2 Timothy 2:15, KJV). It should therefore be our ambition to mimic the Bereans of Paul's time.

> **Now the Bereans were of more noble character than the Thessalonians, for they received the message with great eagerness and examined the Scriptures every day to see if what Paul was saying was true.**
> **–Acts 17:11**

Because of our human frailty, however, we must guard against the inevitable bent toward pride and elitism often borne out of intellectual learning. Without the guidance of the Holy Spirit, and without a humble attitude that seeks to study the Scriptures because of a desire to be conformed to the character of Jesus and be a benefit to the Body of Christ, a head full of knowledge from even this holiest of all books will result only in a proud heart, which always seeks to exalt itself above those who are less informed. This is what the Pharisees of Jesus' time were guilty of. Pride divides the Body of Christ, but humility unites it.

Andrew Murray once wrote:

> *After writing what we have given extracts from [referring to his written Bible teachings], Law goes on to prove how in the Church of Christ the gifts of human learning and wisdom speedily asserted themselves instead of that entire dependence upon the Holy Spirit of which Christ had spoken. And with that learning came, as a natural consequence, the exaltation of self and the whole difference became the question between Pride, in the power of human learning and wisdom, and Humility, in the absolute dependence of the teaching of the Holy Spirit.*

Simply stated, Murray was asserting that without an absolute dependence on the Holy Spirit to illuminate truth and reveal human nature, Bible learning for him became an intellectual exercise only and a breeding ground for pride. How we guard against such an outcome is a subject of too great a depth to explore fully within the limited space of these closing comments.

Suffice it to say that it is our first duty when studying God's Word to apply the teachings therein to ourselves, and secondly to seek to be a benefit to others with the knowledge and wisdom gained from the Scriptures. The latter is what I hope I have achieved for the reader of this book.

Although I hope I have helped to move the two polarized camps a little closer together with this treatise, I would like to reiterate a point I made in the introduction: I realize the very attempt to topple the sacred cow of eternal security will of itself appear somewhat divisive since attempting to discredit a doctrine many hold so dear may be regarded as offensive by some. While unison and love are important to me, unity for unity's sake is not my chief aim if that apparent harmony leaves certain errors and false teachings unaddressed. Therefore, with all due esteem and brotherly affection toward my brethren who hold to an unconditional eternal security doctrine, I must say, respectfully, there is no way to get eternal security out of the Scriptures without seriously distorting them. Therefore, it is only right to declare to these dear souls that what they believe and teach is false doctrine.

There are times when God's people must be bold – in love – and be willing to call out sin and false doctrine wherever it is found, even when it has the potential to offend. Part of the problem in American churches is the discomfort many clergy have in addressing anything uncomfortable or controversial in the hopes of keeping people happy and attending regularly. This leads only to shallow and milk-fed Christians instead of those who are able to take "solid food," as the writer of the book Hebrews declared:

> [11]*We have much to say about this, but it is hard to explain, because you are dull of hearing.* [12]*Although by this time you ought to be teachers, you need someone to reteach you the basic principles of God's word. You need milk, not solid food!* [13]*For everyone who lives on milk is still an infant, inexperienced in the message of righteousness.* [14]*But solid food is for the mature, who by constant use have trained their senses to distinguish good from evil.*
> -Hebrews 5:11-14

I hope what I have presented here will, if nothing else, motivate you to diligently study God's Word for yourself. If that is all I accomplish, then the outcome will be a positive one.

In closing, I would like to again acknowledge there is indeed some healthy tension between the two camps of thinking, and I submit to you that perhaps God designed it this way to let us know He is still God and no one can truly explain Him or His ways to the intellectual satisfaction of finite human beings. God will always make our minds go "tilt," because the human mind is incapable of perfectly understanding the One Who made it. Even so, Ephesians 1:9 tells us God has "*made known to us the mystery of His will according to His good pleasure, which He purposed in Christ.*" While we cannot know every facet of God's infinite nature, there are nevertheless certain things He has made known to us in His Word. I hope this book has helped reveal some of them to you.

I pray God will bless you and enlighten you as you search the Scriptures and seek to do His will. And may He bind us all together with cords of love, humility, and unity.

Bibliography

1. J. Myers. *Jesus Invites You into His Inner Circle of Friends* (Matthew 11:27). RedeemingGod.com.
2. J. Myers. *Paul Does Not Teach Total Depravity in Romans 3.* RedeemingGod.com.
3. *Calvinism vs. Arminianism: Which View is Correct?* GotQuestions.org. No author named.
4. Thomas R. Schreiner. *Does Romans 9 Teach Individual Election Unto Salvation: Some Exegetical and Theological Reflections.* JETS, 36/1 (March 1993) 25-40
5. Greg Boyd. *How Do You Respond to Romans 9?* Jan. 17, 2008. www.reknew.org
6. R. T. Forster and V. P. Marston, *God's Strategy in Human History* (Wheaton: Tyndale, 1973) 67.

Resources

Other books and materials by Andrew Robbins can be accessed at www.AndrewRobbinsMinistries.org and www. BlessedLifeFellowship.org.

Printed in the United States
By Bookmasters